THE LOW FODMAP DIET COOKBOOK

AN ADVANCED IBS RELIEF GUIDE FOR A HEALTHY GUT. 150 EASY, QUICK, AND HEALTHY RECIPES AND A CUSTOM STEP-BY-STEP PLAN TO HELP YOU WITH DIGESTIVE DISORDERS. (VOL.2)

Kirsten McCall

TABLE OF CONTENTS

Introduction

FODMAP consists of various forms of carbohydrates that are located in specific foods such as beans and wheat. There is a strong bond existing between FODMAP and digestive symptoms such as bloating, gas, stomach pain, constipation, and diarrhea. The term FODMAP is used to refer to a chain of carbohydrates (Fermentable, Oligo-, Di, Mono-saccharides, And Polyols). These carbohydrates are short-chain, and they are absorbed poorly in the small intestine. They are made of short-chain disaccharides (lactose). Also oligosaccharides polymers of fructose, (that is, fructans) is part of the short chain followed by monosaccharides (fructose), galactooligosaccharides (GOS) and stachyose (raffinose). Another short chain is sugar alcohols (polyols). The sugar alcohol includes xylitol, mannitol, sorbitol and maltitol. These carbohydrates tend to affect smooth digestion, thereby making the digestive tract resist food. The reason for this because they fail to get absorbed into the bloodstream, and when this happens, they move to the end of the intestine where the bacteria of the gut stay, and they act upon them. These carbs at the location become fuel that make gas (hydrogen). These gas is what leads to digestive symptoms in people with IBS.

Most of the FODMAPs are found naturally in food and the human diet. However, foods and beverages produced artificially for commercials can also contain polyols. People who are hypersensitive to luminal distension are liable to suffer from digestive discomfort as a result of the intake of Fodmap food. However, FODMAPs does not lead to intestinal inflammation, and it has been observed that the FODMAPs produced naturally helps in preventing the possibility of experiencing digestive discomfort because they offer alterations in the gut flora, which are beneficial. In highly sensitive people, FODMAPs can bring liquid closer to the intestine, which leads to diarrhea. People with irritable bowel syndrome are highly sensitive to FODMAPs. A low-Fodmap diet has been an answer that helps to restrict FODMAPs and this aids in the improvement of short-term digestive symptoms that occurs in adults who are suffering from irritable bowel syndrome and any other functional gastrointestinal disorders.

More on FODMAPs

The presence of FODMAPS (especially fructans) is small in grains that contain gluten. They have been categorized as a possible trigger that leads to the symptoms in people suffering from non-celiac gluten sensitivity. When a person eats FODMAPs in the actual standard quantities in a daily diet, FODMAPs have minor sources. However, this bloating is different from the extra-digestive symptoms that people who are not sensitive to non-celiac gluten can experience, including fibromyalgia, neurological disorders, psychological disturbances, and dermatitis. As much as a low-Fodmap diet is great, using it without undergoing a medical evaluation can lead to other health risks. This is because it can mask the digestive symptoms that accompany the celiac disease, by delaying or preventing its real and appropriate diagnosis and therapy.

Chapter 1:
The Low FOMAP Diet

FODMAPs can be found in a wide variety of foods but some foods are more well-known for being high-FODMAP. The following foods are examples of high-FODMAP foods:

Contain **Lactose**: regular and low-fat milk and yogurt; soft cheeses like ricotta, cream cheese, and cottage cheese; ice cream, and custard.

High in **Fructose:** fruits like mangoes, pears, cherries, apples, watermelon, or canned fruits marinated in fruit juices; vegetables like sugar snap peas, asparagus, and artichokes; sweeteners like honey and high-fructose corn syrup.

Contain **Fructans** and **Galacto-oligosaccharides:** grains like wheat, rye, and their products; fruits like watermelon, peaches, and persimmons; vegetables like onions, garlic, artichokes, and legumes (baked beans, kidney beans, etc.); and other products such as inulin—a form of supplemental fiber

Contain **Sorbitol (Polyol):** fruits like apples, blackberries, nectarines, pears, apricots, and plums; beverages like apple juice and pear juice.

Contain **Mannitol (Polyol):** vegetables like cauliflower, sugar snap peas, and mushrooms; fruits like watermelon.

Contain both **Sorbitol and Mannitol (Polyols):** sweet candies like sugar-free gum, some hard candies, and some chocolate.

What Happens When We Eat FODMAPs?

Since FODMAP molecules are so resistant to digestion, they are not easily absorbed into the bloodstream. In fact, they can travel unchanged throughout the entire length of the intestine and can encourage different parts of your digestive system to draw more water than necessary from your bloodstream. This can result in runny and watery bowel movements in individuals whose systems are sensitive to FODMAPs.

As mentioned above, FODMAP molecules can travel all the way to the end of the digestive tract where most good and helpful gut bacteria, or microflora, reside. There, the bacteria are unsure of what to do with the high amounts of undigested carbs, so they use the molecules as fuel. This respiration process (biological process of producing energy from organic substances) results in the production of excess byproducts, like hydrogen gas, that can cause more indigestion symptoms.

Since FODMAPs themselves are not harmful (only people with FODMAP sensitivities experience any kind of negative symptoms), intolerances depend largely on the quantity of food you eat. You can compare this phenomenon to any other food or drink. For example, drinking 5 gallons of water would most definitely kill you, but sticking to ½ or 1 gallon a day would keep you as healthy as a horse. The toxicity of the different things you ingest change as the quantities of those things changes as well. Thus, it is important to recognize that FODMAPs can wreak havoc on your system if you are not being aware of how much of each ingredient you are eating.

As I mentioned, FODMAPs themselves are not inherently bad, and scientists have found that most people who have a sensitivity to FODMAPs are, more likely than not, people with IBS. It is important to recognize that different FODMAPs can affect different IBS sufferers in different ways.

Who Should Follow the Low-FODMAP Diet?

Studies have shown that following a low-FODMAP diet can help alleviate the symptoms and extreme discomfort that IBS sufferers feel on a day-to-day basis. Though the diet is adapted for IBS sufferers, there are parts of the low-FODMAP diet that will also help reduce food-related discomfort for people who have mild gluten or dairy intolerances.

If you have noticed that stress causes your bowel movements to change or increases the chances of you having stomach pain or cramps, you might want to try stress management as a treatment for IBS. However, if you have been practicing stress management techniques, but you don't see a definite decrease in the intensity and frequency of your IBS symptoms, I would highly suggest giving the low-FODMAP diet a chance. Although it is not for everyone, the low-FODMAP diet has shown in many studies that it helps reduce your daily symptoms and can help you return to a normal life when other methods are less effective.

To sum up, you should certainly give the low-FODMAP diet a go if you suffer from chronic and severe gut problems from IBS. I recommend you give this diet a sincere try, and I hope that you will see positive results!

What Is IBS?

IBS, or irritable bowel syndrome, is a condition that affects about 15% of the global population. It is also known by other more descriptive names, including irritable colon, spastic colitis, and mucous colitis. Although similarly named, IBS differs greatly from IBD, inflammatory bowel disease, which is an autoimmune condition that causes chronic inflammation and other issues along the entirety of the digestive tract. Aside from being painful and extremely disruptive, IBD can be life-threatening. Therefore, if you feel you may have IBD and not IBS, please see a doctor for your condition.

Classic IBS presents as a group of symptoms from the intestine, including abdominal pain or discomfort and changes in bowel habits, including frequency and form changes. In order to be diagnosed, these symptoms generally must last for at least 3 months and must occur at least 3 times a week. Although a good number of people with IBS experience on and off phases in their symptoms rather than persistent problems, symptoms can become chronic and much harder to control. A doctor may put you on the low-FODMAP as part of his or her diagnosis; if the diet seems to alleviate your symptoms, the doctor will feel more comfortable diagnosing you with IBS. If the diet does not seem to work for you, your doctor will likely test you for food allergies, infection, or celiac disease (gluten intolerance). If you have already been diagnosed with IBS, this book will help you follow the low-FODMAP diet, reduce uncomfortable gut symptoms, and potentially lose weight all at the same time!

Although IBS can affect all people, it most commonly occurs in individuals under the age of 50, and it is twice as common in women as it is in men. Women tend to experience worsened symptoms during or around the time they are menstruating. Some women may even confuse IBS symptoms with PMS. For example, IBS can cause lower back aches, more painful menstruation and menstrual cramps, and fatigue. Although all of these symptoms are, in some way, related to gut malfunction, there are several links between the severity of IBS and the progress of a woman through her childbearing years. It is important to reach out to your doctor if you feel that your symptoms are worsened during your menstrual period because it could be an indicator of another gynecological or gut-related problem. Although the exact relationship between a woman's digestive system and her reproductive system is still unclear, IBS is, for the most part, very similar between men and women.

IBS also seems to have a genetic component attached to it. If a family member has IBS and you begin to experience similar symptoms, it could be linked to the ways the nerves in your digestive tract function. IBS within a family can also point to risk factors in the common environment and lifestyles.

IBS can range from extremely mild to severe. Most people don't ever get treatment or see a doctor for their symptoms, but for individuals who experience frequent, severe symptoms, their quality of life can potentially become quite poor. IBS is an extremely unpredictable disorder, and the wide variety of symptoms can occur at any time and can sometimes have no causal link between anything you ate and the symptoms you experience. Doctors will generally diagnose an individual with IBS if two or more of the following characteristic symptoms are present as a long-term occurrence:

Abdominal Pain and Cramping: Abdominal Pain and Cramping: Abdominal pain cramping that becomes less severe or subsides entirely after a bowel movement is the most common symptom among all IBS sufferers. IBS cramping can be distinguished from other abdominal cramps you may experience because IBS cramps will always result in one of the following three scenarios: changes in stool consistency or color, changes in the frequency of bowel movements, and some pain relief after a bowel movement.

We possess some helpful "good" bacteria in our gut that release signals to the brain and gut in order to help smooth bowel function to occur. Among IBS sufferers, these signals are lost or distorted and lead to irregular function of the muscles along the digestive tract. This leads to pain and muscle cramps in the middle and lower abdomen.

Constipation: Constipation: 50% of all IBS sufferers are afflicted with constipation-predominant IBS. Constipation or having less than three-bowel movements a week is a common symptom of many ailments, but IBS-related constipation is different because it is generally accompanied by abdominal pain. Constipation is the result of nerve and gut signals that slow transit of materials and stool throughout the digestive tract. When this happens, the bowel continues to absorb more and more water from the stool, making it even harder to pass. This condition is also characterized by the feeling of an incomplete or excessively strained bowel movement.

Diarrhea: Roughly 33% of all IBS sufferers are afflicted with diarrhea-predominant IBS. In this type of IBS, stool is generally watery and tends to lead to very loose motions. Stools can even contain extra mucus from the digestive tract. Diarrhea-predominant IBS sufferers tend to experience an average of 12 bowel movements a week, and those movements can be sudden and extremely difficult to control. As with constipation-predominant IBS, this diarrhea is accompanied by pain that subsides after a bowel movement. Sudden-onset diarrhea can cause mental health repercussions as patients develop anxiety about their bowel movements and are held back from engaging in activities they are worried about.

Alternating Constipation and Diarrhea: Alternating Constipation and Diarrhea: Approximately 20% of IBS sufferers experience this type of mixed bowel movement routine. This type of IBS is again characterized by chronic and recurrent abdominal pain, but sufferers experience more intense and frequent symptoms. The phases of each type of bowel movement can last for days or weeks and can unpredictably switch at any time, regardless of whether the individual's diet is consistent or suddenly changing.

Gas and Bloating: As we have seen, IBS causes a variety of digestive inconsistencies. This can lead to excess gas production in the gut, and the resulting uncomfortable bloating can become chronic. If gas, bloating, and pain are the most prevalent symptoms you experience with your IBS, a low-FODMAP diet is the most effective way to help reduce your discomfort.

Unlike IBD, scientists and doctors are still unable to pinpoint the exact cause of IBS. They have, however, identified some factors that do seem to play an important role in the symptoms many people experience.

Miscommunication between the nervous system and gut: The brain and gut work together to encourage smooth and regular bowel movements. If the signals between the brain and gut become uncoordinated, stool movement throughout the intestines can slow down or become excessively accelerated.

Stress: This is a major trigger for most IBS sufferers because it alters the way the nervous system performs daily functions. Since nervous system functionality and its ability to properly communicate is so important to regular gut function, stress generally worsens IBS symptoms. High-FODMAP foods can also worsen IBS symptoms because of the extra gases they introduce to the body system. This generally leads to abdominal discomfort.

Malfunction in the colon: Sometimes, your colon can respond to different triggers by alternating between slow and spastic muscular movements that can damage tissue and cause painful cramping in your abdomen. Serotonin molecules can also collect in excessive amounts in the colon (most likely another effect of miscommunication between the brain and gut, as described above) and can lead to changes in the muscular motility and resulting bowel movements. Finally, if you have mild celiac disease that is undiagnosed, you could be causing more harm to your intestines, which, in turn, could lead to a variety of IBS symptoms.

Since IBS is a chronic illness, treatments are geared toward long-term symptom management and not necessarily toward a concrete cure. IBS sufferers are, first and foremost, encouraged to discover and avoid their personal IBS triggers. Thus, as a general rule, individuals who are diagnosed with IBS are generally told to follow some form of the low-FODMAP diet and try and minimize the major stressors in their lives so they can experience a pain-free and more predictable life. Some doctors also recommend peppermint oil to help relax the bowel and types of therapy to help limit stress. If these "home-remedies" do not help make a significant positive impact on your quality of life as it relates to IBS, your doctor may look into putting you on prescription medication for your symptoms. In this book, we will be focusing on the benefits of the low-FODMAP diet and ways to follow it!

How Does the Low-FODMAP Diet Work?

Low-FODMAP should be restrictive only for a short amount of time in order to avoid deficiency in some essential nutrients. We will delve more into how to maintain good nutrition while on the diet. For now, we will discuss how the diet works and the three steps that you should take to help the diet benefit you as much as possible. The low-FODMAP diet is generally divided into three phases where each has different limitations and goals. They are described below:

Phase 1: Elimination. This is the time when you will follow the low-FODMAP to a T and I encourage you to explore and follow all the recipes in this book during this phase. This phase will be the toughest one because you are limiting your high-FODMAP intake. This phase should last between 2-8 weeks depending on your body's response, and you should try not to stay on this restrictive diet for much longer than that.

During this phase, you will eliminate all high-FODMAP foods from your diet and stick to a strict serving size for all ingredients and foods to ensure you are only eating foods in the low-FODMAP range. Remember that elimination is referring only to FODMAPs and you should not be eliminating entire food groups from your diet. Instead you should aim to think of this diet as a substitution diet where you replace high-FODMAP foods with low-FODMAP foods, like replacing an apple a day with an orange a day. This does in fact eliminate high-FODMAP foods from your diet but still helps you maintain balance and nutrition.

Phase 2: Reintroduction. This phase should begin straight after the previous phase and should be planned while your elimination phase is still ongoing. It might be scary to start reintroducing foods back into your diet, particularly if the elimination phase considerably reduced your IBS symptoms. After 2-8 weeks of eliminating high-FODMAP foods and substituting low-FODMAP foods in their place, you should begin introducing reasonable amounts of high-FODMAP foods back into your diet, one subcategory at a time. This way, you give your body time to adjust to reintroduction and you will easily be able to tell which new foods are still intolerable to you.

As you are beginning to eat these foods again, the rest of your diet should remain low-FODMAP so that you can isolate the high-FODMAP foods you are eating. This phase can take up to 6-8 weeks, depending on how many foods you wish to try bringing back into your daily diet and should be done in a methodical way. Take your time with this phase, as it will be extremely helpful when you move onto the next phase and try to maintain a fully tolerable diet for yourself.

Phase 3: Maintenance. This is the "final" phase of the low-FODMAP diet, and it is when you have the freedom to personalize the diet so that you can maintain it long term. You should only begin maintaining your ideal diet once you have fully identified and interpreted your trigger foods and the quantities you can tolerate other foods.

This phase involves allowing your diet to go as close to normal as possible so that you are only controlling the intake of specific foods that trigger your IBS symptoms. It is important to note that a bowel afflicted with IBS can change unpredictably and cause you to become intolerant of foods you used to take well, and vice versa. If this happens, talk with your nutritionist and maybe try going through phase 2 again to identify your new triggers and tolerances. Eventually, you should be able to tolerate most high-FODMAP foods (again, in reasonable quantities) without setting off your IBS.

It is important to have a wide diet range, so please make sure to follow these three phases as best as you can. Our goal at the end of the low-FODMAP diet is to have hopefully expanded your diet and not further restricted it.

Chapter 2:
The Low FODMAP Diet
Meal Plan

Following is a 28-day meal plan for basic IBS, listing recipes found in the book. Remember to include one or two healthy snacks per day to control hunger. Shopping lists can be found

WEEK 1

DAY	BREAKFAST	LUNCH	DINNER	DESSERT
1	Blueberry & Seed Smoothie Bowl	Minestrone	Salmon Fritters With Vermicelli Noodles	Low-Fodmap Brownies
2	Ginger-Lemon Zinger Smoothie	Cheesy Chicken Fritters	Spinach, Pumpkin And Tomato Muffins	Low-Fodmap Lemon Bar
3	Coconut-Cinnamon Colada Smoothie	Crispy Falafel	Sweet Red Pepper Soup	Low-Fodmap Butterscotch
4	Pumpkin Spice Smoothie	Hawaiian Toastie	Rustic Chicken Saagwala	Low-Fodmap Cookies
5	Raspberry-Vanilla Smoothie	Chicken Alfredo Pasta Bake	Beef Stew	Low-Fodmap Cupcake
6	Simple Steel Cuts	Kabocha Squash Soup	Instant Picadillo	Almost Classic Hummus
7	Vanilla Flavored Oats	Easy Beef Curry	Spicy Beef Chilies	Carrot Dip

WEEK 2

DAY	BREAKFAST	LUNCH	DINNER	DESSERT
8	Feta Baked Eggs	Beef And Carrots	Beef Steak Soup	Minty Melon Mélange
9	Buckwheat Porridge	Korean Beef Ribs	Almond Butter And Beef	Citrusy Salsa
10	Cherry And Farro Bowl	Rosemary Beef Stew	Delicious Corned Beef	Rainbow Salsa
11	Sausage Breakfast Stacks	Shrimp With Beans	Arugula Grapes Salad	Low-Fodmap Brownies
12	Spicy Breakfast Scramble	Broccoli Fritters	Veggie Pasta Bean Soup	Low-Fodmap Lemon Bar
13	Bacon-Jalapeño Egg Cups	Roasted Broccoli	Tasty Cilantro Lime Green Rice	Low-Fodmap Butterscotch
14	Bacon And Egg Cauliflower Hash	Roasted Maple Carrots	Apple Carrot Kale Salad	Low-Fodmap Cookies

WEEK 3

DAY	BREAKFAST	LUNCH	DINNER	DESSERT
15	Bacon, Spinach, And Avocado Egg Wrap	Sweet & Tangy Green Beans	Perfect Asian Salad	Low-Fodmap Cupcake
16	Blueberry & Seed Smoothie Bowl	Minestrone	Salmon Fritters With Vermicelli Noodles	Almost Classic Hummus
17	Ginger-Lemon Zinger Smoothie	Cheesy Chicken Fritters	Spinach, Pumpkin And Tomato Muffins	Carrot Dip
18	Coconut-Cinnamon Colada Smoothie	Crispy Falafel	Sweet Red Pepper Soup	Minty Melon Mélange
19	Pumpkin Spice Smoothie	Hawaiian Toastie	Rustic Chicken Saagwala	Citrusy Salsa
20	Raspberry-Vanilla Smoothie	Chicken Alfredo Pasta Bake	Beef Stew	Rainbow Salsa
21	Simple Steel Cuts	Kabocha Squash Soup	Instant Picadillo	Low-Fodmap Brownies

WEEK 4

DAY	BREAKFAST	LUNCH	DINNER	DESSERT
22	Vanilla Flavored Oats	Easy Beef Curry	Spicy Beef Chilies	Low-Fodmap Lemon Bar
23	Feta Baked Eggs	Beef And Carrots	Beef Steak Soup	Low-Fodmap Butterscotch
24	Buckwheat Porridge	Korean Beef Ribs	Almond Butter And Beef	Low-Fodmap Cookies
25	Cherry And Farro Bowl	Rosemary Beef Stew	Delicious Corned Beef	Low-Fodmap Cupcake
26	Sausage Breakfast Stacks	Shrimp With Beans	Arugula Grapes Salad	Almost Classic Hummus
27	Spicy Breakfast Scramble	Broccoli Fritters	Veggie Pasta Bean Soup	Carrot Dip
28	Bacon-Jalapeño Egg Cups	Roasted Broccoli	Tasty Cilantro Lime Green Rice	Minty Melon Mélange

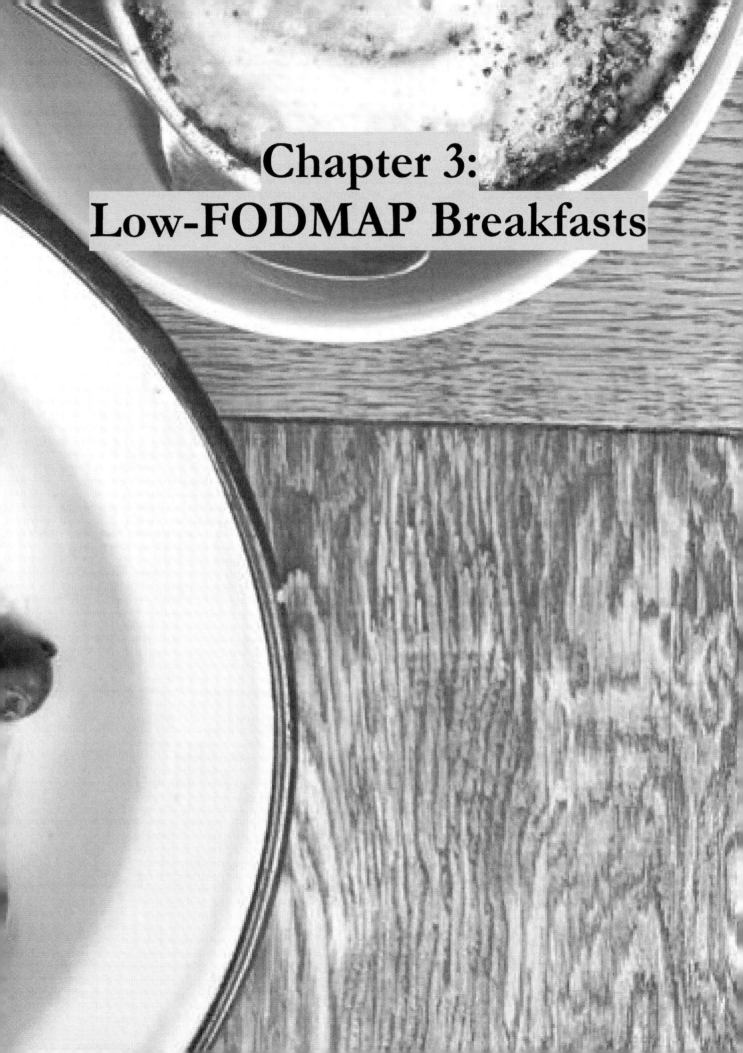

Chapter 3:
Low-FODMAP Breakfasts

1.   Blueberry & Seed Smoothie Bowl

Preparation Time: 10 minutes   **Cooking Time:** 0 minutes   **Servings:** 1

Ingredients:

½ banana, frozen   ½ cup fresh blueberries   ¼ teaspoon ground turmeric
½ tablespoon flaxseed   ¼ cup mixed berries, frozen   ½ tablespoon raw pumpkin seeds
1 tablespoon unsweetened shredded coconut
1 cup water or unsweetened nut milk or canned coconut milk

Directions:

In a blender, combine the spinach, frozen berries, banana, water, turmeric, flaxseed, and pumpkin seeds. Blend until smooth but not runny—it should be thick. Pour the smoothie into a bowl, top creatively with fresh blueberries and coconut shreds.

STORAGE NOTE: Best consumed immediately.

RECIPE TIP: Adding ice instead of water will keep the smoothie thick and cold.

Nutrition:

Calories: 254 kcal   Cholesterol: 0 mg   Fiber: 80 g
Total Fat: 12 g   Sodium: 32 mg   Sugar: 0 g
Saturated Fat: 8 g   Total Carbs: 34 g   Protein: 6 g

2. Ginger-Lemon Zinger Smoothie

 Preparation Time: 5 minutes

 Cooking Time: 0 minutes

Servings: 1

Ingredients:

½ lemon

1 cup ice cubes

1 cup water or unsweetened nut milk or coconut milk

1 cup romaine lettuce

1 green apple, quartered

¼ teaspoon ground turmeric

½ inch fresh ginger root, peeled

Directions:

In a blender, combine the ginger, turmeric, lemon, apple, romaine, water, and ice. Blend on high for at least 1 minute. Add more water and blend some more if the consistency is too thick for your taste. Pour into a glass and enjoy.

STORAGE NOTE: Best consumed immediately. You can store this smoothie in an airtight container after you make it, but it should be consumed within an hour for maximum flavor and health benefits.

RECIPE TIP: This smoothie can be a powerful detoxifier, and you may feel some tummy rumbling after drinking it. Don't worry; that's completely normal.

Nutrition:

Calories: 137 kcal

Total Fat: 1 g

Saturated Fat: 0 g

Cholesterol: 0 mg

Sodium: 6 mg

Total Carbs: 36 g

Fiber: 7 g

Sugar: 0 g

Protein: 1 g

3. Coconut-Cinnamon Colada Smoothie

Preparation Time: 5 minutes

Cooking Time: 0 minutes

Servings: 1

Ingredients:

1 cup ice

1 cup frozen pineapple

¼ teaspoon ground cinnamon, plus more for garnish

½ cup coconut milk, full fat

¼ cup plain goat or dairy kefir

Directions:

In a high-powered blender, combine the ice, pineapple, kefir, coconut milk, and cinnamon. Blend until smooth. Pour into a tall glass, top with a dash of extra cinnamon, and enjoy.

STORAGE NOTE: This smoothie will keep, covered with a lid, for 24 hours in the fridge. Give it a good shake before drinking after storing. However, it's best consumed immediately.

RECIPE TIP: This refreshing smoothie can be poured into ice pop molds and frozen for delicious summer treats.

Nutrition:

Calories: 382 kcal

Total Fat: 30 g

Saturated Fat: 26 g

Cholesterol: 0 mg

Sodium: 43 mg

Total Carbs: 31 g

Fiber: 5 g

Sugar: 0 g

Protein: 5 g

4. Raspberry-Vanilla Smoothie

Preparation Time: 5 minutes

Cooking Time: 0 minutes

Servings: 1

Ingredients:

1 cup ice

½ cup Greek yogurt

2 scoops vanilla protein or collagen powder (I love Vital Proteins vanilla coconut collagen)

1 teaspoon raw honey

1 cup frozen raspberries

½ teaspoon vanilla extract

1 inch fresh ginger root, peeled

Directions:

In a blender, combine the raspberries, Greek yogurt, ginger, ice, vanilla, protein powder, and honey. Blend for at least 1 minute, or until smooth. Pour into a tall glass and enjoy.

STORAGE NOTE: Best enjoyed immediately. You can store in the fridge in an airtight container for a few days; shake well before consuming.

RECIPE TIP: If you are not tolerating dairy well, you can use unsweetened coconut yogurt instead of the Greek yogurt here.

Nutrition:

Calories: 271 kcal

Total Fat: 1 g

Saturated Fat: 0 g

Cholesterol: 0 mg

Sodium: 222 mg

Total Carbs: 29 g

Fiber: 8 g

Sugar: 0 g

Protein: 38 g

5. Feta Baked Eggs

Preparation Time: 5 minutes

Cooking Time: 10 minutes

Servings: 4

Ingredients:

4 slices feta

4 whole eggs

1 cup of water

1 tablespoon olive oil

2 spring onions, chopped

1 tablespoon cilantro, chopped

Directions:

The original breakfast dish, simple feta dressed baked eggs! Grease 4 ramekins with oil and sprinkle green onion in each. Crack an egg into each and top with cilantro and cheese. Add water to your Pot. Place a steamer basket. Place ramekin inside and cover. Cook on LOW pressure for 4 minutes. Release pressure naturally. Serve and enjoy!

Nutrition:

Calories: 170 kcal

Total Fat: 11 g

Saturated Fat: 3 g

Cholesterol: 0 mg

Sodium: 0 mg

Total Carbs: 13 g

Fiber: 2 g

Sugar: 2 g

Protein: 8 g

6. Cherry And Farro Bowl

Preparation Time: 10 minutes

Cooking Time: 40 minutes

Servings: 4

Ingredients:

¼ cup chives

2 cups of water

¼ teaspoon salt

½ cup dried cherries, coarsely chopped

1 tablespoon olive oil

2 cups cherries, pitted

1 teaspoon lemon juice

1 cup whole grain Farro

8-10 mint leaves, minced

1 tablespoon apple cider vinegar

Directions:

If you like adding cherries to your dish, then this Farro bowl is what you need! Rinse your Farro and add them to your Instant Pot alongside 2 cups water. Lock up the lid and cook on HIGH pressure for 40 minutes. Quick-release the pressure. Drain the Farro and transfer to a bowl. Stir in vinegar, lemon juice, oil, dried cherries, mint, salt, chives. Chill and stir in the fresh cherries. Enjoy!

Nutrition:

Calories: 250 kcal

Total Fat: 10 g

Saturated Fat: 3 g

Cholesterol: 0 mg

Sodium: 0 mg

Total Carbs: 20 g

Fiber: 6 g

Sugar: 8 g

Protein: 8 g

7. Scrambled Tofu

Preparation Time: 5 minutes

Cooking Time: 5 minutes

Servings: 4

Ingredients:

1 cup water
1 lb. pre-pressed tofu, firm

1 teaspoon ground turmeric
2 cup carrots, chopped finely

4 teaspoon gluten-free soy sauce
1 tablespoon garlic infused olive oil

Directions:

Use a glass dish to blend turmeric, soy sauce, and water until integrated. Scrub carrots and chop into small sections. Transfer to the dish. Break apart tofu into smaller sections into the dish, then toss to combine fully. Empty garlic-infused olive oil into a skillet and warm over the medium setting of heat. Distribute the mixture into the pan and toss occasionally while it heats for 5 minutes. Remove with a slotted spoon and serve immediately. Enjoy!

Nutrition:

Protein: 19g
Carbohydrates: 11g

Fat: 13g
Sodium: 137g

Fiber: 4g
Calories: 224

8. Spicy Breakfast Scramble

 Preparation Time: 5 minutes   **Cooking Time:** 10 minutes   **Servings:** 2

Ingredients:

6 large eggs

2tablespoons ghee

Pink Himalayan salt

Freshly ground black pepper

2 tablespoons heavy (whipping) cream

½ cup chopped scallions, white and green parts

6 ounces Mexican chorizo or other spicy sausage

½ cup shredded cheese, like pepper Jack, divided

Directions:

A breakfast scramble is one of those meals you can make with a variety of ingredients. This one is inspired by Mexican flavors, but you can just as easily make one with Italian- or Mediterranean-inspired flavors. The Mexican chorizo, a spicy sausage, provides the zesty meat base to this scramble, and with creamy eggs, cheese, and scallions, this easy breakfast will keep you satisfied for hours. I use pepper Jack cheese for extra spice. In a large skillet over medium-high heat, melt the ghee. Add the sausage and sauté, browning for about 6 minutes, until cooked through. In a medium bowl, whisk the eggs until frothy. Add the cream, and season with pink Himalayan salt and pepper. Whisk to blend thoroughly. Leaving the fat in the skillet, push the sausage to one side. Add the egg mixture to the other side of the skillet and heat until almost cooked through, about 3 minutes. When the eggs are almost done, mix in half of the shredded cheese. Mix the eggs and sausage together in the skillet. Top with the remaining shredded cheese and the scallions. Spoon onto two plates and serve hot.

VARIATIONS: To take this scramble to the next level, you can add some toppings that will elevate the flavor profile and add healthy fat: Top the scramble with ½ sliced avocado, a diced jalapeño, and a dollop of sour cream. Top the scramble with 1 tablespoon of salsa, 1 tablespoon of sliced black olives, and 1 tablespoon of chopped fresh cilantro leaves.

SUBSTITUTION TIP: If you can't find Mexican chorizo, you can use regular ground beef and spices like garlic powder, cumin, and oregano.

Nutrition:

Calories: 850 kcal

Total Fat: 70 g

Saturated Fat: 0 g

Cholesterol: 0 mg

Sodium: 0 mg

Total Carbs: 7 g

Fiber: 1 g

Sugar: 0 g

Protein: 46 g

9. Quinoa Tofu Scramble

Preparation Time: 5 minutes

Cooking Time: 15 minutes

Servings: 4

Ingredients:

2 cups spinach
¼ teaspoon black pepper

8 oz. pre-pressed tofu, firm
½ teaspoon turmeric powder

½ teaspoon iodized salt, separated
3 teaspoons garlic infused olive oil

Direction:

Ensure the quinoa is properly rinsed under cold water. Transfer to a deep pot and blend ¼ teaspoon of salt with water. Heat on the highest setting until the fluid is starting to bubble, then turn the burner temperature down. Warm for an additional 12 minutes or until fluid is fully reduced. In the meantime, set out a skillet and empty garlic-infused olive oil to start warming. Rinse spinach well and shake to remove excess moisture. Set aside. Break tofu into small sections and put it into the pan. Combine the leftover ¼ teaspoon of salt, turmeric, and black pepper until fully incorporated. Warm the mixture on the stove for approximately 3 minutes while continuously tossing. Toss in spinach and continue to stir continuously for an additional 2 minutes. Layer quinoa and tofu scramble into each serving dish. Serve immediately and enjoy!

Nutrition:

Protein: 9g
Carbohydrates: 3g

Fat: 8g
Sodium: 311g

Fiber: 2g
Calories: 117

10. Bacon-Jalapeño Egg Cups

 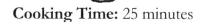

Preparation Time: 5 minutes   **Cooking Time:** 25 minutes   **Servings:** 6

Ingredients:

For the Bacon:

6 bacon slices

1 tablespoon butter

For the Eggs:

4 large eggs

2 jalapeño peppers

Pink Himalayan salt

Freshly ground black pepper

¼ cup shredded Mexican blend cheese

2 ounces cream cheese, at room temperature

Directions:

To make the Bacon: Bacon egg cups are the perfect keto breakfast, snack, or even side dish. The crispy bacon on the outside, mixed with the creamy egg middle and spicy jalapeño, will start your day with a kick. The cream cheese mixed with bits of jalapeño pepper provides just the right amount of heat. Preheat the oven to 375°F. While the oven is warming up, heat a large skillet over medium-high heat. Add the bacon slices and cook partially, about 4 minutes. Transfer the bacon to a paper towel−lined plate. Coat six cups of a standard muffin tin with the butter. Place a partially cooked bacon strip in each cup to line the sides. To make the Eggs: Cut one jalapeño lengthwise, seed it, and mince it. Cut the remaining jalapeño into rings, discarding the seeds. Set aside. In a medium bowl, beat the eggs with a hand mixer until well beaten. Add the cream cheese and diced jalapeño, season with pink Himalayan salt and pepper, and beat again to combine. Pour the egg mixture into the prepared muffin tin, filling each cup about two-thirds of the way up so they have room to rise. Top each cup with some of the shredded cheese and a ring of jalapeño, and bake for 20 minutes. Cool for 10 minutes, and serve hot.

SUBSTITUTION TIP: If you don't have jalapeños available, or you don't like spicy food, you can use bell peppers or another vegetable with a little crunch, like asparagus.

Nutrition:

Calories: 159 kcal

Total Fat: 13 g

Saturated Fat: 0 g

Cholesterol: 0 mg

Sodium: 0 mg

Total Carbs: 1 g

Fiber: 0 g

Sugar: 0 g

Protein: 9 g

11. Fish Wallpaper with Green Bean Salad

Preparation Time: 5 minutes

Cooking Time: 15 minutes

Servings: 4

Ingredients:

1 teaspoon salt
4 pieces of fish
4 pinches of salt
2 cups of tomato

1 cup of green bean
1/2 cup of lemon juice
4 teaspoons of olive oil
4 pieces of serrano chili
1 clove of roasted garlic

4 tablespoons fresh coriander
1/4 cup epazote cut into strips
1 piece of roasted habanero chili
4 pieces of yellow lemon cut into slices
1/2 piece of spring onion cut into strips

Directions:

Preheat the oven to 360 °F. Add the tomato, yellow lemon juice, habanero pepper, garlic and salt to the blender. Blends perfectly well. Spread an aluminum foil with waxed paper on top add the fish and garnish with the olive oil, add the salt, the sauce, the slices of lemon, the onion, the Chile, the coriander, and the epazote. Close and bake around 20 minutes. Inside a pot with boiling water and add salt, cook the green beans 5 minutes until they are cooked: drain and reserve Now, serve the fish, add green beans, season with olive oil and add salt to it.

Nutrition:

Calories   96.1 kcal
Carbohydrates   18.4 g

Proteins   5.9 g
Lipids   0.6 g

Dietary fiber   7.2 g
Sugars   4.7 g

12. Tomato and basil frittata

Preparation Time: 10 minutes

Cooking Time: 25 minutes

Servings: 4

Ingredients:

10 large eggs
113 g. baby spinach leaves
15 ml. Paleo or butter cooking fat
15 ml. whole or homemade mustard
Sea salt with freshly ground black pepper to add taste

Fresh basil leaves to taste (to garnish)
1 large spring onion, cut into thin slices
2 small ripe tomatoes cut into thin slices
5 slices of bacon, sliced into small pieces

Directions:

Preheat the oven to 360°F. Beat the eggs and mustard in a bowl and season to taste. Heat the cooking fat in an oven-proof frying pan over medium heat. Cook the bacon and the onion until the onion is golden brown (approximately 5 to 6 minutes). Add the spinach into the pan and cook for another minute or until the spinach is wilted. Pour the egg mixture into the pan. Cook until it hardens a little and places the tomatoes on top. Once the edges well cook the frittata, but still dripping in the center, put the pan into the oven till the frittata takes a nice golden color. Garnish with some basil leaves on top and serve.

Nutrition:

Carbohydrates 11g   Dietary Fiber 1g   Protein 8g

13. Lettuce Tacos with Chicken to the Shepherd

Preparation Time: 1,5 Hours

Cooking Time: 35 minutes

Servings: 6

Ingredients :

1 tablespoon salt marinade

1/2 cup chopped coriander

1 tablespoon of olive or flax oil

Enough of French Lettuce Eva

3 garlic cloves for the marinade

2 pieces of clove for the marinade

1/2 cup finely chopped purple onion

50 grams of achiote for the marinade

1/2 cup pineapple juice for marinade

1 tablespoon cumin for the marinade

1 tablespoon fat pepper for marinade

1 tablespoon oregano for the marinade

1/4 piece of white onion for the marinade

1/4 cup of apple vinegar for the marinade

1/2 piece of pineapple cut into half moons

1 piece of roasted guaje tomato, for the marinade

1 piece of boneless and skinless chicken breast, cut into small cubes

2 pieces of wide chili clean, deveined and seedless, hydrated for the marinade

3 pieces of guajillo Chile clean, deveined and seedless, hydrated for the marinade

To the taste of lemon to accompany

To the taste of tree chili sauce to accompany

Directions:

For the marinade, blend the achiote, vinegar, chilies, garlic, onion, juice, salt, pepper, cloves, oregano, tomato, and cumin until a homogeneous mixture is obtained. Put the chicken and the marinade inside a bowl with the shepherd marinade for 1 hour in refrigeration. Heat a pan over medium heat with the oil and cook the chicken you marinated until it is cooked. Reserve covered. Heat a grill over high heat, roast the pineapple until golden brown, remove and cut into cubes, reserve. On a table place sheets of French Lettuce Eva add the chicken to the shepherd and serve with the roasted pineapple, cilantro, onion, served with a little sauce and lemons.

Nutrition:

Calories   92.2 kcal

Carbohydrates   22.3 g

Cholesterol   0.0 mg

Proteins   1.6 g

Lipids   0.9 g

Dietary fiber   2.9 g

Sugars   6.6 g

14. Green Apple Salad with Garbanzo

Preparation Time: 10 minutes

Cooking Time: 2 minutes

Servings: 1

Ingredients:

1 pinch of salt

1 pinch of pepper

1/4 cup strawberry

1 cup chopped arugula

2 teaspoons of olive oil

1/4 cup of toasted chickpea

2 cups chopped Eva Lettuce

3 tablespoons of raspberry vinegar

1 cup of green apple cut into thin slices

Directions:

In a bowl add the lettuce, the arugula, add the green apple, with the chickpea. Mix perfectly well. Reservation. Add the olive oil with the strawberry, salt, pepper and raspberry vinegar to the blender. Blends perfectly well. Serve the salad on a plate and add the strawberry vinaigrette to garnish. Enjoy

Nutrition:

Calories   878 kcal

Carbohydrates   122 g

Cholesterol   0.0 mg

Proteins   36.2 g

Lipids   34.1 g

Dietary fiber   36.5 g

Sugars   50.3 g

15. Sheet Pan Steak Fajitas

Preparation Time: 10 minutes

Cooking Time: 25 minutes

Servings: 4

Ingredients:

3 tablespoons olive oil
2 teaspoons chili powder
2 teaspoons ground cumin
4 to 5 cloves garlic, minced
1 teaspoon smoked paprika
Salt and black pepper, to taste

1 spring onion, cut into wedges
1 green bell pepper, cut into strips
1 orange bell pepper, cut into strips
2 tablespoons freshly squeezed lime juice
680 grams sirloin steak, cut into thin strips
6 (8-inch) flour, corn tortillas or carb balance, warmed

Directions:

Preheat oven to 425 °F. Lightly oil a baking sheet or coat with nonstick spray. In a small bowl, combine chili powder, cumin, paprika, 2 teaspoons salt and 2 teaspoons pepper. Place steak, bell peppers, onion and garlic in a single layer onto the prepared baking sheet. Stir in olive oil and chili powder mixture; gently toss to combine. Place into oven and bake for 25 minutes, or until the steak is completely cooked through and the vegetables are crisp-tender. Stir in lime juice. Serve immediately with tortillas.

Nutrition:

Calories 440 kcal
Fat 33g
Carbohydrates 5g

Fiber 1g
Sugar 1g
Protein 31g

Vitamin C 78.4 mg
Iron 3.7 mg

16. Sheet Pan Tuscan Chicken

Preparation Time: 10 minutes

Cooking Time: 25 minutes

Servings: 4

Ingredients:

1 cup Olive Oil
1 teaspoon Salt
2 Tablespoons Parsley

1-pound Green Beans
5 cloves Garlic, Minced
1 onion, cut into chunks
1 teaspoon Black Pepper

1/3 cup Balsamic Vinegar
1 teaspoon Dried Parsley Flakes
4 wholes Boneless, Chicken Thighs
6 whole Roma Tomatoes, quartered

Directions:

To a bowl or pitcher, add the olive oil and balsamic vinegar, along with the garlic, parsley, salt, and pepper. Whisk it until it's well blended. Place the chicken in a large zipper bag and pour in half the dressing. Seal the bag and set it aside. Cut the tomatoes in quarters. Cut onion into chunks. Trim the ends off the green beans, and place the veggies in a large zipper bag. Pour in the rest of the dressing, then seal the bag and set them aside. Preheat the oven to 425 °F Arrange the chicken and veggies on a sheet pan, Pour a little of the marinade on top of the chicken. Roast in the oven for 25 minutes, shaking the pan once during that time.

VARIATION TIP: With a few minutes left of cook time, lay slices of fresh mozzarella on each chicken breast. Return them to the oven until melted. Sprinkle ½ cup shredded Parmesan all over the pan as soon as you remove it from the oven. Let it sit a few minutes before serving.

Nutrition:

Calories 441 kcal
Fat 22g
Saturated Fat 5g
Cholesterol 119mg

Sodium 986mg
Potassium 1044mg
Carbohydrates 15g
Fiber 3g

Sugar 8g
Protein 43g
Calcium 215mg
Iron 2.7mg

17. Sheet Pan Egg in the Hole

Preparation Time: 10 minutes

Cooking Time: 20 minutes

Servings: 6

Ingredients:

6 large eggs
6 slices bread

12 slices bacon
Red pepper flakes, to taste
Butter, at room temperature

6 tablespoons Mozzarella cheese
2 tablespoons chopped fresh chives
Salt and freshly black pepper, to taste

Directions:

Preheat oven to 400 °F. Place bacon in a single layer onto a baking sheet. Place into oven and bake until par-cooked, about for 5-7 minutes. Transfer to a paper towel-lined plate. Lightly oil a baking sheet or coat with nonstick spray. Cut a 3-inch hole in the center of each bread slice. Butter one side of the bread slices. Place the bread onto the prepared baking sheet, buttered side down. Add bacon slices and eggs, gently cracking the eggs into each hole and keeping the yolk intact. Sprinkle with Parmesan and red pepper flakes; season with salt and pepper, to taste. If your bacon is too thick, cut it in half so the egg can sink into the hole. Place into oven and bake until the egg whites have set about 12-15 minutes. Serve immediately, garnished with chives, if desired.

Nutrition:

Calories 292.0
Total Fat 19.0g
Saturated Fat 9.5g

Cholesterol 223.0mg
Sodium 700.0mg
Total Carbohydrate 13.0g

Dietary Fiber 1.0g
Protein 15.0g

Chapter 4:
Low-FODMAP Entrees

18. Herb-Stuffed Pork Loin Roast

Preparation Time: 20 minutes   **Cooking Time:** 2 Hours   **Servings:** 10

Ingredients:

Rock salt
120 grams leek
200 grams risotto rice
1 tablespoon olive oil

10 grams green onions
½ teaspoon thyme, dried
1 teaspoon oregano, dried
500 milliliters chicken stock

1 cup fresh parsley, chopped
2.5 kilograms pork loin roast
3 tablespoons pumpkin seeds
1 tablespoon garlic-infused oil

Directions:

Remove the white stems of the leeks and chop the green tips. Do the same with the green onions. Put the green tips of the leek in a large saucepan. Cook in garlic-infused oil and olive oil over medium heat for about 2 minutes. Add rice into the saucepan and stir for a minute. Pour 125 milliliters of the chicken stock into the rice and leek mixture. Stir occasionally. Reduce heat to medium low. Continue adding chicken stock in batches while stirring until the rice is cooked. Remove from heat once done. Add parsley, pumpkin seeds, green onions, thyme and oregano to the rice. Put the risotto in a bowl and set aside to cool. Use a sharp knife to make ½ inch deep slices on the pork skin that are 1/2 inch apart. Stuff the pork loin with the rice mixture and tie it properly. Coat with olive oil and season with salt. Roast pork in a preheated oven at 220 degrees Celsius for 30 minutes. Sprinkle the pork juices over the roast a few times during the cook. Reduce the heat to 200 degrees Celsius and return the pork roast to the oven and cook for another 1 ½ hour. Drizzle the meat juices over the roast every 30 minutes. Allow to rest for 10 minutes before serving.

Nutrition:

Calories: 434 kcal
Total Fat: 14.2 g
Saturated Fat: 0 g

Cholesterol: 0 mg
Sodium: 0 mg
Total Carbs: 20.5 g

Fiber: 0.6 g
Sugar: 0.7 g
Protein: 56.1 g

19. Low Fodmap Stuffing

Preparation Time: 10 minutes

Cooking Time: 30 minutes

Servings: 12

Ingredients:

¼ teaspoon sea salt
1 teaspoon sage, dried
½ teaspoon thyme, dried

¼ teaspoon black pepper
1 teaspoon oregano, dried
125 milliliters chicken stock
4 tablespoons butter, melted

1 tablespoon garlic-infused oil
10 slices wheat bread, shredded
13 grams fresh parsley, chopped
120 grams green leek leaves, chopped

Directions:

Set the oven to 180 degrees Celsius. Mix garlic-infused oil and butter. Coat bread pieces with oil mixture. Arrange the bread in a baking tray. Cook in the oven for 5 minutes. Turn the bread and bake for another 5 minutes. Remove from oven. Place bread in a bowl with the remaining ingredients. Mix well.

Nutrition:

Calories: 120 kcal
Total Fat: 5.6 g
Saturated Fat: 0 g

Cholesterol: 0 mg
Sodium: 0 mg
Total Carbs: 14.8 g

Fiber: 0.9 g
Sugar: 1.6 g
Protein: 3 g

20. Chili Coconut Crusted Fish

Preparation Time: 15 minutes

Cooking Time: 45 minutes

Servings: 4

Ingredients:

460 grams cod

4 kaffir lime leaf, sliced

1 tablespoon sesame oil

57 grams cheddar cheese, grated

20 grams dried coconut, shredded

10 grams green onion leaves, sliced

1 mild green chili, deseeded and sliced

Directions:

Soak coconut in water for 10 minutes. Remove excess water. Fry chili, green onions and lime leaves in 1 tablespoon sesame oil over medium-high heat. Once fragrant, add coconut and cook for another minute. Remove from heat and set aside for later. Fry the fish for 2 minutes on each side. Transfer fish to a baking tray. Sprinkle cheese on top and coat with coconut mixture. Grill on high in the oven for 2 minutes.

Nutrition:

Calories: 227 kcal

Total Fat: 10.8 g

Saturated Fat: 0 g

Cholesterol: 0 mg

Sodium: 0 mg

Total Carbs: 1.4 g

Fiber: 0.7 g

Sugar: 0.5 g

Protein: 30 g

21. Spicy Chicken Drumsticks

Preparation Time: 10 minutes

Cooking Time: 45 minutes

Servings: 4

Ingredients:

¼ teaspoon paprika
1 teaspoon coriander
¼ teaspoon cloves, ground

¼ teaspoon cumin, ground
8 pieces chicken drumsticks
½ teaspoon turmeric, ground

2 tablespoons garlic-infused oil
1 ½ tablespoon pure maple syrup
½ teaspoon black pepper, ground
½ teaspoon yellow mustard powder

Directions:

Combine oil and maple syrup together in a bowl. Mix the dried spices in a separate bowl. Rub each chicken with the oil mixture then completely coat with the spice rub. Bake chicken in a preheated oven at 180 degrees Celsius for 45 minutes.

Nutrition:

Calories: 492 kcal
Total Fat: 31.1 g
Saturated Fat: 0 g

Cholesterol: 0 mg
Sodium: 0 mg
Total Carbs: 2.4 g

Fiber: 0.2 g
Sugar: 1.5 g
Protein: 46.1 g

22. Paprika Calamari With Garden Salad

 Preparation Time: 5 minutes   **Cooking Time:** 10 minutes   **Servings:** 5

Ingredients:

Salt

Dressing

Olive oil

Garden Salad

½ teaspoon salt

1 small head romaine lettuce, roughly chopped

⅓ cup cornstarch

1 teaspoon paprika

1 cup snow pea shoots

½ teaspoon Stevia extracts

2 stalks celery, thinly sliced

1½ tablespoons lemon juice

2 tablespoons garlic-infused olive oil

½ green bell pepper, seeded and sliced

½ teaspoon finely ground black pepper

4 large or 8 regular squid bodies, cleaned

½ large cucumber halved lengthwise and sliced

Directions:

Slice the squid bodies down to two large pieces (slice them into quarters if you use big squid). Cut the squid bits in a 1/2-inch (1 cm) cross pattern with a sharp knife, making sure it is not cut through all the time. Pat dry on towels of paper. Combine the pepper, paprika, salt, and corn starch in a fairly large bowl and mix thoroughly. Cover for 3 to 4 hours and cool. To cook the salad, combine in a large salad bowl the shoots of latch, cucumber, celery, snow pepper, and snow pea. In order to dress in the size of the dressing, add prune puree, lemon juice, and Stevia extracts. Taste salt for season. Preheat the grill to warm or heat a saucepan or grill over high temperatures. Brush with oil the grill or bowl. Add the calamari, rate, and cook for 2 to 3 minutes. Turn and cook for another 1-2 minutes until the squid is opaque in white. Wash the dressing and spread the salad into four bowls or plates. Arrange and serve the calamari warm on top.

Nutrition:

Calories: 229.2 kcal

Total Fat: 15.1 g

Saturated Fat: 2.2

Cholesterol: 264.1 mg

Sodium: 50.9 mg

Total Carbs: 5.1 g

Fiber: 0.1 g

Sugar: 0.3 g

Protein: 17.8 g

23. Chili Salmon With Cilantro Salad

Preparation Time: 5 minutes

Cooking Time: 10 minutes

Servings: 5

Ingredients:

Cilantro Salad
2 tablespoons lime juice
2 tablespoons fish sauce
1 tablespoon rice vinegar

2 tablespoons Stevia extracts
Four 5½-ounce salmon fillets
½ green bell pepper, thinly sliced
½ small red chile, finely chopped
Salt and freshly ground black pepper

5 cups roughly chopped lettuce leaves
½ cup firmly packed chopped cilantro
1 tablespoon garlic-free sweet chili sauce
2 stalks celery, thinly sliced on the diagonal
½ large cucumber halved lengthwise and sliced

Directions:

Line the broiler with the sheet of foil and put the oven in the grill 5 inches away. Place the fillets of salmon in the crust, skin-side up, and coat until crispy for 1 to 2 minutes. Try turning on the fillets and brush the sweet chili sauce with 3/4 teaspoon. Salt and pepper season. Season. Alternatively, fry for 3 to 4 minutes or until properly cooked. Mix the celery, bell pepper, lettuce, cucumber, and cilantro together in a big bowl to make the salad. In a small bowl, add the chili, the lime juice, rice vinegar, the fish sauce, and the Stevia extracts. Serve with fish.

Nutrition:

Calories: 293.7 kcal
Total Fat: 14.2 g
Saturated Fat: 2.8 g

Cholesterol: 80.8 mg
Sodium: 366.2 mg
Total Carbs: 1 g

Fiber: 0 g
Sugar: 0.2 g
Protein: 38.9 g

24. Dukkah-Crusted Snapper

Preparation Time: 5 minutes

Cooking Time: 10 minutes

Servings: 4

Ingredients:

Dukkah	Cooked basmati rice	½ teaspoon chili powder
Cilantro leaves	1 teaspoon cumin seeds	½ cup blanched almonds
Lemon wedges	2 tablespoons canola oil	1 teaspoon ground coriander
¼ cup pine nuts	1 teaspoon sesame seeds	Four 7-ounce snapper fillets or other lean fish

Directions:

Preheat oven to 330°F when preparing the dukkah and line the parchment paper on a baking sheet. Place almonds and pine nuts on the baker and bake 5 minutes or until golden. Bake for 5 minutes. Refrigerate to room temperature. In a food processor, put all nuts and spices and pulse until the crumbs have been thin. Retention of four tablespoons and pass the remainder to a pot. Brush the fillets with gasoline, drive them all over to cover the dukkah. Thermally heat a grilled grill or cast iron saucepan. Add the fish and cook on each side for 3 to 4 minutes before frying. Sprinkle the coriander and the dukkah reserved. Serve with rice basmati and wedges of lemon.

Nutrition:

Calories: 580 kcal	Cholesterol: 110 mg	Fiber: 10 g
Total Fat: 23 g	Sodium: 410 mg	Sugar: 16 g
Saturated Fat: 9 g	Total Carbs: 60 g	Protein: 38 g

25. Balsamic Sesame Swordfish

Preparation Time: 5 minutes

Cooking Time: 15 minutes

Servings: 4

Ingredients:

Steamed Asian greens

4 large swordfish steaks

2 tablespoons soy sauce

2 tablespoons Stevia extracts

1½ tablespoons sesame seeds

3 tablespoons balsamic vinegar

Directions:

In a non-metallic dish, mix balsamic, soy, and Stevia extracts. Attach the steaks of swordfish and transform the marinade into coat. Cover and cool, turn periodically for 3-4 hours. To 450 ° F, preheat the oven line a large parchment paper baking sheet. Place the steaks of swordfish on a bakery book and book the marinade for 10 minutes. Turn over the steaks and add the marinade. Sprinkle with sesame seeds and cook until cooked for another 5 to 10 minutes. Serve with the Asian greens steamed.

Nutrition:

Calories: 95 kcal

Total Fat: 11 g

Saturated Fat: 1 g

Cholesterol: 0 mg

Sodium: 122 mg

Total Carbs: 0 g

Fiber: 0 g

Sugar: 0 g

Protein: 0 g

26. Lemon-Oregano Chicken Drumsticks

Preparation Time: 10 minutes

Cooking Time: 15 minutes

Servings: 4

Ingredients:

Greek Salad

4 ounces feta

2 tablespoons olive oil

½ cup pitted kalamata olives

2 teaspoons balsamic vinegar

18 skinless chicken drumsticks

¼ cup finely chopped oregano

12 cherry tomatoes, cut in half

2 cups shredded iceberg lettuce

2 tablespoons extra virgin olive oil

Salt and freshly ground black pepper

1 tablespoon finely grated lemon zest

Directions:

Use a little knife to evenly pierce the chicken. In a large bowl, add the oregano, citrus fruit, and oil. Add the chicken, salt, and pepper season and cover with the meat. Cover, cool, turn periodically for 3 to 4 hours. To 450 ° F, preheat the oven cover two parchment paper bakery boards. Place the drumsticks on the slabs and cook until golden brown and cooked for 10 to 15 minutes. In the meantime, put the salad in a large bowl and gently toss the lettuce, tomatoes, olives, and feta. Place the olive oil and vinegar in a tiny glass and blend well. Place the salad over and throw it quickly. Eat with chicken, with the extra oregano. Serve.

Nutrition:

Calories: 35 kcal

Total Fat: 35 g

Saturated Fat: 0 g

Cholesterol: 0 mg

Sodium: 470 mg

Total Carbs: 2 g

Fiber: 0 g

Sugar: 0 g

Protein: 0 g

27. Low Fodmap Carrot & Corn Fritters

Preparation Time: 10 minutes

Cooking Time: 20 minutes

Servings: 4

Ingredients:

2-large egg
1 ½-tsp paprika
2-tbsp fresh parsley

240g-(2 large) carrot
½-tsp ground cumin
Carrot & corn fritters
1-red bell peppers (large)

12g-(1/4 cup) fresh chives
128g-(3/4 cup) sweet corn
63ml-(1/4 cup) low fodmap milk
70g-(1/2 cup) gluten free all-purpose flour

Directions:

Mesh the carrots, deseed and dice the crimson ringer peppers, and degree out the corn quantities. Nicely cleave the chives and parsley. In a big bowl mix the eggs and espresso milk (fodmap) together. Whilst you are carried out with that mixture inside the flour, paprika, and cumin. Mix the corn, carrot, pink ringer peppers, chives, and parsley until they form. Season with salt and pepper. Spot a massive non-stick fry container over medium warm temperature and shower with oil. Spoon 1/four cup combo for each waste into the container. Cook 4 to six wastes one after some other-leveling them marginally so they are not very thick. Permit to cook dinner for 3 to 4mins for every aspect, till extremely good dark-colored and cooked through. Ensure you blend the blend before cooking each bunch. Serve 3 wastes for everybody.

Nutrition:

Calories: 187 kcal
Total Fat: 4 g
Saturated Fat: 0 g

Cholesterol: 0 mg
Sodium: 0 mg
Total Carbs: 30.8 g

Fiber: 0 g
Sugar: 8.2 g
Protein: 7.4 g

28. Low Fodmap Hawaiian Toasties

Preparation Time: 4 minutes

Cooking Time: 6 minutes

Servings: 1

Ingredients:

30g-shaved ham
35g-cheddar cheese
40g-canned pineapple chunks in syrup (drained weight)

Season with black pepper
2-slices low fodmap bread

1 tablespoon dairy free spread
1 tablespoon green onions/scallions

Directions:

Preheat medium frypan over medium warmth. Spread the outside of the low fodmap bread. Mesh the cheddar and cut the ham. Channel, wash and finely hack the tinned pineapple. Finely slash the green tips of the green onions/scallions. Collect your cheddar toasties. Make certain to put buttered sides outwardly, at that point include the cheddar, ham, pineapple, green onions/scallions and a sprinkle of dark pepper. Cook each side for around 3 minutes until brilliant darker. Serve hot, unwind, and appreciate!

Nutrition:

Calories: 454 kcal
Total Fat: 26.5 g
Saturated Fat: 0 g

Cholesterol: 0 mg
Sodium: 0 mg
Total Carbs: 33.7 g

Fiber: 0 g
Sugar: 3 g
Protein: 19.9 g

Chapter 5:
Low-FODMAP Appetizers

29. Low-Fodmap Tomato Bruschetta

Preparation Time: 5 minutes

Cooking Time: 5 minutes

Servings: 3

Ingredients:

A pinch of sea salt

3 medium tomatoes

1 teaspoon of dried basil

1 teaspoon of dried chives

2 teaspoons of balsamic vinegar

Half a teaspoon of dried oregano

1 teaspoon of balsamic reduction

2 tablespoons of extra virgin olive oil

Directions:

To begin, rinse your tomatoes with tepid water, deseeded, then chop them. Put the tomatoes into a medium sized mixing bowl, then add the vinegar, spices, reduction, and olive oil, stir to combine, then season with salt (more if needed). Set aside to marinate for 30 minutes. Serve with crackers or baguettes with a drizzle of balsamic reduction.

Nutrition:

Calories: 130 kcal

Total Fat: 6 g

Saturated Fat: 0 g

Cholesterol: 0 mg

Sodium: 0 mg

Total Carbs: 19 g

Fiber: 0 g

Sugar: 2 g

Protein: 7 g

30. Low-Fodmap Cheese Bread

Preparation Time: 12 minutes

Cooking Time: 30 minutes

Servings: 8

Ingredients:

2 eggs

1 teaspoon of sea salt

2 cups of tapioca Flour

Half a cup of coconut oil

1 cup of lactose free milk

1 cup of parmesan cheese

Directions:

Preheat your oven to 450°F. Pour the milk into a medium-sized saucepan, set over medium heat and bring to a slow boil. Once bubbles start to form at the top of the milk, remove from heat. Pour the tapioca flour into the milk, stir using a wooden ladle until all the flour is incorporated and no lumps are formed and the mixture starts to thicken like gelatin, then set aside to cool for a bit. Beat the dough for a couple of minutes at medium speed using a standing mixer fitted with a paddle attachment. Crack the egg into a small bowl and whisk until foamy, then slowly fold them into the dough, make sure to scrape down the sides of the bowl. Add the cheese and beat until fully incorporated and your dough is stretchy, soft and sticky. Line a baking sheet with parchment paper, then scoop some dough into it using an ice cream scoop. Coat your hands or ice cream scoop with some olive oil if the dough gets too sticky to work with. Place the baking sheet into the preheated oven and allow the dough to bake for 25-30 minutes. Remove from the oven once the top of the bread appears dry and starts to show orange flecks of color.

Nutrition:

Calories: 160 kcal

Total Fat: 13.7 g

Saturated Fat: 0 g

Cholesterol: 0 mg

Sodium: 0 mg

Total Carbs: 16.3 g

Fiber: 0 g

Sugar: 7 g

Protein: 19 g

31. Low-Fodmap Spring Rolls

Preparation Time: 15 minutes   **Cooking Time:** 40 minutes   **Servings:** 5

Ingredients:

Filling;

1 carrot
1 turnip
1 zucchini
Rice paper

1 cup of cilantro
Half a cup of mint
Half a cup of basil
12 medium-sized shrimps

Marinate;

1 teaspoon of fish sauce
A pinch of white Pepper
1 tablespoon of coconut oil
1 tablespoon of scallions (green part only)

2 teaspoons of chopped ginger
2 teaspoons of gluten free soy sauce
1 tablespoon of garlic infused olive oil

Peanut Sauce;

2 teaspoons of fish sauce
1 teaspoon of dried chilli flakes
2 teaspoons of natural cane syrup
¼ cup of natural smooth peanut butter (sugar free)

2 tablespoons of wheat free soy sauce
2 tablespoons of garlic infused olive oil
2 tablespoons of freshly squeezed lime juice

Directions:

To marinate the shrimp; Put all the marinade ingredients into a ziplock bag, add the shrimps (make sure they are fully covered) then refrigerate for a little over 30 minutes. Put all the peanut sauce ingredients into a large mixing bowl, stir with a wooden ladle until well combined. Cut up or julienne the turnip, carrot and zucchini. Put the coconut oil into a large skillet and saute all the ingredients (except mint and basil leaves) for the following for 1-2 minutes (do not overcook).

To make the spring rolls; Dip the rice paper into a large bowl of water for 3-5 seconds until it softens a bit, then remove it and a bit of all the vegetables, cilantro and shrimp, then break the mint leaves and basil by hand and put them in the rolls. Fold in the sides, then gently roll the wraps and voila! Your very own Low-FODMAP spring rolls!

NOTE: You really have to work fast with the rice paper as they get really sticky when wet and tend to break apart as they lose moisture. So, tick tick goes the clock!

Nutrition:

Calories: 279 kcal
Total Fat: 8 g
Saturated Fat: 0 g

Cholesterol: 0 mg
Sodium: 0 mg
Total Carbs: 12 g

Fiber: 0 g
Sugar: 2 g
Protein: 24 g

32. Low-Fodmap Cucumber Bites

 Preparation Time: 30 minutes

 Cooking Time: 0 minutes

 Servings: 20

Ingredients:

2 cucumbers

1 tablespoon of roasted paprika
Half a cup of lactose-free cream cheese

Half a cup of Low-FODMAP egg salad
Half a cup of Low-FODMAP tuna salad

Directions:

Chop the cucumbers into round bite-sized pieces, then use a spoon to make a small groove in the middle. Scoop some egg salad over a third of the cucumber slices, then the tuna salad over another third and the cream cheese over the rest, taking care not to over top them lest they start to fall off. Drain and cut the roasted paprika into small pieces, then top the cream cheese with the roasted paprika and serve.

Nutrition:

Calories: 159 kcal
Total Fat: 9 g
Saturated Fat: 0 g

Cholesterol: 0 mg
Sodium: 0 mg
Total Carbs: 4 g

Fiber: 0 g
Sugar: 2.1 g
Protein: 11.9 g

33. Low-Fodmap Salmon Cakes

Preparation Time: 10 minutes

Cooking Time: 40 minutes

Servings: 2

Ingredients:

1 lemon zest
2 medium carrots

A can of wild salmon
Pepper and salt to taste

A handful of chives (chopped)
Half a tablespoon of coconut oil
Half a tablespoon of coconut flour

Directions:

Preheat your oven to 400F. Line a baking sheet with pieces of parchment paper. Peel and chop the carrots, then put them into a food processor, pulse until the carrots are small and well diced up. Open the can of salmons and drain it of all liquid, then set aside. Add the rest of the ingredients into the food processor, along with the salmons, pulse until well combined and almost smooth. Use your hand to form the mixture into palm-sized cakes, using a paper towel to pat any excess liquid. Gently place the newly formed cakes onto your baking sheet and place them in the oven. Bake for 40 minutes or more if you want them a bit crispy. Serve warm.

Nutrition:

Calories: 226 kcal
Total Fat: 13.8 g
Saturated Fat: 0 g

Cholesterol: 0 mg
Sodium: 0 mg
Total Carbs: 25 g

Fiber: 0 g
Sugar: 3 g
Protein: 6.5 g

34. Feta, Pumpkin, And Chive Fritters

Preparation Time: 5 minutes

Cooking Time: 10 minutes

Servings: 4

Ingredients:

⅓ cup fine rice flour
½ cup chopped chives
Garden Salad, optional

2 tablespoons canola oil
2 tablespoons cornstarch
½ teaspoon xanthan gum
3 tablespoons light sour cream

Pumpkin or other winter squash
Salt and freshly ground black pepper
½ to 1 teaspoon ground cumin (to taste)
½ cup crumbled feta 2 eggs, lightly beaten

Directions:

Cook the pumpkin 8-10 minutes, until tender, in a medium saucepan of boiling water. Drain and mix. Reserve to be refreshing. Sift rice flour (or blend with a whisk to make sure they are properly combined), cornstarch, and xanthan gum in the large mixing bowl. Attach 2 cabbage teaspoons, feta, cups, eggs, and cumin, and blend together well. Add salt and pepper to taste. Burn up 1 tablespoon of oil over medium heat in a fairly large non-stick skillet. Apply 2 tablespoons of heaping batter to frying and cook for 2-3 minutes. Flip through the back of a spatula and flatten slightly, then cook for a further 2 minutes, or until crispy golden, and then brown. Move the chips to a plate and cover them with foil to warm them if you intend on eating it right away (save them for later on in the fridge). Keep in mind to cook all fritters with remaining oil and batter. Blend the sour cream together and 1 tablespoon of cabbage left. If wanted, match the fritters with salad and a dollop of sour cream.

Nutrition:

Calories: 294 kcal
Total Fat: 15 g
Saturated Fat: 0 g

Cholesterol: 0 mg
Sodium: 0 mg
Total Carbs: 28 g

Fiber: 0 g
Sugar: 0 g
Protein: 9 g

35. Chicken Tikka Skewers

Preparation Time: 5 minutes   **Cooking Time:** 10 minutes   **Servings:** 4

Ingredients:

Garden Salad

¾ cup Greek yogurt

2 teaspoons turmeric

¼ teaspoon ground cumin

1 tablespoon garam masala

¼ teaspoon ground coriander

1 tablespoon finely grated ginger

Salt and freshly ground black pepper

¼ to ½ teaspoon chili powder (to taste)

2½ pounds boneless skinless chicken breast

Directions:

In a large bowl, mix the garam masala, cumin, chili, yogurt, ginger, coriander and turmeric, and salt and potato. Incorporate the pieces of chicken and marinade until evenly coated. Cover with a wrap of plastic and cool 2 hours. Preheat broiler. Load the chicken in 18 skewers. Place on the broiler or baking sheet, and grill until golden, brown, and just cooked for 6 to 8 minutes on every side. Serve with salad.

Nutrition:

Calories: 178 kcal

Total Fat: 1 g

Saturated Fat: 0 g

Cholesterol: 0 mg

Sodium: 0 mg

Total Carbs: 5 g

Fiber: 0 g

Sugar: 0 g

Protein: 13 g

36. Tuna, Lemongrass, And Basil Risotto Patties

 Preparation Time: 10 minutes

 Cooking Time: 15 minutes

 Servings: 4

Ingredients:

Canola oil

½ cup cornstarch

¾ cup arborio rice

2 tablespoons chopped basil

2 eggs, lightly beaten, divided

3 cups onion-free chicken stock

1⅓ cups gluten-free bread crumbs

Salt and freshly ground black pepper

2 tablespoons finely chopped lemongrass

One 5-ounce can oil-packed tuna, drained

Directions:

In a large cup, pour the stock and bring to a boil. Incorporate the rice and let it cook until tender for 10-12 minutes. Drain excess fluid. Stir in the salmon, citrus fruit, and basil while still dry and blend well together. Switch to a medium bowl and keep cool until room temperature is reached. Preheat the oven to 150 degrees C (300 degrees F). In the cooled rice, add 1 beaten egg and 1/3 cup (40 g), salt, and pepper to taste. Shape 8 large balls into a mixture and flatten them to make pats. Place the majority of the maize starch and the remainder of one cup (120 g) of bread crumbs into three small bowls. (When the mixture is not quite firm enough, add more bread crumbs.) Coat the patties with maize, then beat the egg and eventually crumbs. Set the plate aside. Heat oil over medium-high heat in a medium saucepan. In the pot, add 4 patties, and cook on both sides for 2-3 minutes, until browned evenly. Take a baker and keep warm in the fireplace. Cook the remaining patties in the pot with a little more oil. Serve with salad.

Nutrition:

Calories: 54 kcal

Total Fat: 1 g

Saturated Fat: 0 g

Cholesterol: 59 mg

Sodium: 108 mg

Total Carbs: 1 g

Fiber: 0 g

Sugar: 0 g

Protein: 8 g

37. Cheese-And-Herb Polenta Wedges With Watercress Salad

Preparation Time: 10 minutes

Cooking Time: 15 minutes

Servings: 4

Ingredients:

4 cups watercress
½ red bell pepper
½ green bell pepper

½ cup grated parmesan
⅓ Cup chopped oregano
⅓ Cup chopped marjoram
3 tablespoons alfalfa sprouts

½ small cucumber, thinly sliced
1/3 cup chopped flat-leaf parsley
3 cups onion-free vegetable stock
3 tablespoons lemon-infused olive oil

Directions:

In a medium casserole, bring the stock to a boil. Put polenta in and cook for 3 to 5 minutes over medium heat and stir continuously, making the mix very dense. Add Parmesan, oil and grasses (20 g) to the mixture. Let the polenta cool down and leave it in the fridge for an hour. Preheat the oven to 180°C and fill in a baking sheet of parchment paper. Place the polenta on a cutting board and cut it into eight coils or rectangles. Sprinkle with the remaining Parmesan onto the wedges in the baking sheet. Bake the cheese for about 10 to 15 minutes until it has melted, and the wedges are somewhat white. Combine cucumber, green, watercress, and red bell peppers, and lukewarm sprouts in a large bowl to make the watercress salad. Drizzle and mix together with a lemon-infused oil. Serve on soft wedges of polenta.

Nutrition:

Calories: 284.1 kcal
Total Fat: 12.6 g
Saturated Fat: 6.3 g

Cholesterol: 34.8 mg
Sodium: 329.9 mg
Total Carbs: 24.1 g

Fiber: 3.5 g
Sugar: 0.7 g
Protein: 19.9 g

38. Spiced Tofu Bites

Preparation Time: 10 minutes

Cooking Time: 25 minutes

Servings: 6

Ingredients:

Cooked rice
Garden Salad
½ teaspoon salt

¼ teaspoon paprika
1/3 cup vegetable oil
¼ teaspoon ground allspice

14 ounces puffed tofu pieces
1 teaspoon ground caraway seeds
½ teaspoons freshly ground black pepper

Directions:

In a small bowl, mix the seeds of salt, paprika, caraway pepper, and allspice, then add 2 tablespoons of the oil. Brush the mixture of spice over the tofu and pass it to a plate. Cover with a lid and wait for 2 to 3 hours for the flavors to blend together. In a medium-high saucepan, heat the remaining oil. Fill the tofu and cook on each side for 1 to 2 minutes, until warm. Serve with rice and salad steamed.

Nutrition:

Calories: 134.8 kcal
Total Fat: 7.3 g
Saturated Fat: 1.1 g

Cholesterol: 0 mg
Sodium: 1992.3 mg
Total Carbs: 5.9 g

Fiber: 1.1 g
Sugar: 1 g
Protein: 14.6 g

Chapter 6:
Low-FODMAP Lunches

39. Minestrone

Preparation Time: 10 minutes

Cooking Time: 40 minutes

Servings: 4

Ingredients:

Olive oil

80 grams leek

Salt and pepper

50 grams celery, sliced

65 grams middle bacon

60 grams spinach, sliced

160 grams potato, diced

240 grams carrots, diced

160 grams zucchini, diced

12 gr fresh basil, chopped

310 milliliters boiling water

2 tablespoons garlic-infused oil

3 tablespoons parmesan cheese

75 grams shell pasta, gluten-free

400 g canned plain tomatoes, chopped

500 ml low FODMAP vegetable stock

168 g canned chickpeas, rinsed and drained

Directions:

Remove the white stem of the leeks. Chop the green tips finely and set aside. Slice the bacon into small pieces after removing the rind. Over medium heat, saute carrots, potato, leeks, bacon and celery in a large saucepan using garlic-infused oil for about 20 minutes. Add tomatoes, boiling water, chickpeas, vegetable stock, spinach and zucchini into the pan. Turn down the heat to medium-low and let it simmer. After 10 minutes, put the pasta and basil in the pan. Allow the pasta to cook in the soup. Sprinkle salt and pepper to taste. Adjust the soup's consistency by adding water, if desired. Serve with parmesan cheese, baby basil leaves and an extra drizzle of garlic-infused oil.

Nutrition:

Calories: 386 kcal

Total Fat: 17 g

Saturated Fat: 0 g

Cholesterol: 0 mg

Sodium: mg

Total Carbs: 50.4 g

Fiber: 10.6 g

Sugar: 11.8 g

Protein: 11.9 g

40. Cheesy Chicken Fritters

Preparation Time: 10 minutes

Cooking Time: 20 minutes

Servings: 4

Ingredients:

Olive oil
2 large eggs
Black pepper

¼ teaspoon salt
60 milliliters mayonnaise
2 teaspoons chives, dried

500 grams chicken, ground
35 grams plain flour, gluten-free
2 tablespoons fresh basil, chopped
84 grams mozzarella cheese, grated

Directions:

Mix all of the ingredients thoroughly in a large bowl. Season with salt and pepper. Place a large frying pan with olive oil over medium heat. Scoop about ¼ cup of the chicken mixture and place it in the pan. Flatten the mixture slightly using a spatula and let it cook for about 4 minutes on each side. Line a plate with paper towel. Once cooked thoroughly, transfer the fritters into the plate to remove excess oil. Repeat the process for the remaining chicken mixture.

Nutrition:

Calories: 415 kcal
Total Fat: 26.8 g
Saturated Fat: 0 g

Cholesterol: 0 mg
Sodium: 0 mg
Total Carbs: 11.4 g

Fiber: 0.4 g
Sugar: 1.7 g
Protein: 31.3 g

41. Crispy Falafel

Preparation Time: 10 minutes

Cooking Time: 25 minutes

Servings: 5

Ingredients:

80 grams leek

Salt and pepper

2 teaspoons paprika

2 tablespoons olive oil

¾ teaspoon cumin, ground

Zest and juice of 1 large lime

2 tablespoons garlic-infused oil

25 grams fresh parsley, chopped

120 grams carrots, grated and peeled

5 tablespoons plain flour, gluten-free

168 gr canned chickpeas, rinsed and drained

182 gr microwavable brown rice, pre-cooked

Directions:

Set the oven to 190 degrees Celsius. Prepare a roasting tray lined with baking paper. Remove the white stems of the leek and chop the green tips roughly. Except for the plain flour, blend all of the ingredients using a food processor. Once the mixture becomes a smooth paste, add the plain flour and mix well. Use 1 tablespoon of olive oil to grease the baking paper. Form small falafel patties using a tablespoon and place them on the roasting tray. Make sure to allocate enough space between each patty. Coat the top of the patties with olive oil. Place the tray in the oven and cook for about 12 minutes on each side.

Nutrition:

Calories: 187 kcal

Total Fat: 7.1 g

Saturated Fat: 0 g

Cholesterol: 0 mg

Sodium: 0 mg

Total Carbs: 27.7 g

Fiber: 4.5 g

Sugar: 3.6 g

Protein: 4.4 g

42. Chicken Alfredo Pasta Bake

Preparation Time: 10 minutes

Cooking Time: 50 minutes

Servings: 4

Ingredients:

Olive oil

Salt and pepper

5 tablespoons butter

20 grams green onions

750 milliliters rice milk

½ teaspoon basil, dried

450 grams chicken breast

180 grams broccoli florets

240 grams pasta, gluten-free

¼ cup plain flour, gluten-free

120 grams baby spinach, chopped

114 grams cheddar cheese, grated

3 tablespoons fresh sage, chopped

3 tablespoons parmesan cheese, grated

Directions:

Heat the oven to 180 degrees Celsius. Apply olive oil on a large oven dish to grease it. Slice the chicken breast fillet into small pieces. Sear the chicken using olive oil in a large frying pan over medium-high heat. Once the meat is golden brown, remove it from the flame and set aside for later. Remove the white stems of the green onions and chop the green tips finely. Place the spinach leaves in a hot pan until slightly wilted. Remove from heat and place it on one side for later use. Over medium heat, melt the butter in a medium-sized saucepan. Add plain flour into the saucepan and stir continuously for a minute while cooking. Once slightly frothy, add ½ cup of milk into the saucepan and stir until smooth. Pour 1 cup of milk at a time into the mixture while stirring continuously. Season to taste. Add parmesan cheese, basil and 57 grams of cheddar cheese into the sauce. Give the mixture an occasional stir until it gained a thick consistency. Prepare a large saucepan of boiling water and cook the pasta. After 5 minutes, drain the pasta and drizzle with olive oil. Add Alfredo sauce, broccoli, chicken and spinach into the pasta and mix well. Transfer everything to the greased oven dish and sprinkle the remaining cheese on top. Let it cook in the oven for 10 minutes without cover. Place the pasta bake in an oven grill and cook for another 3 minutes. Garnish with sage.

Nutrition:

Calories: 743 kcal

Total Fat: 29.9 g

Saturated Fat: 0 g

Cholesterol: 0 mg

Sodium: 0 mg

Total Carbs: 78.8 g

Fiber: 10 g

Sugar: 11.4 g

Protein: 41 g

43. Rosemary Beef Stew

Preparation Time: 10 minutes

Cooking Time: 20 minutes

Servings: 4

Ingredients:

3 pounds beef
2 teaspoons salt
Water as needed

8 ounces shallots
2 sprigs rosemary
2 carrots, chopped

1 tablespoon olive oil
2 tablespoons almond flour
1 tablespoon almond butter

Directions:

While many people don't really like the flavor of the Rosemary, the balance here is just too perfect to ignore! It's awesome in all the right places. Set the pot to Sauté mode and add olive oil, allow the oil to heat up. Add butter and chopped rosemary and stir. Add shallots, carrots and sauté for a while. Shove the veggies on the side and add the meat cubes, brown them slightly and pour just enough stock to gently cover them, season with salt. Lock up the lid and cook on 20 minutes on HIGH pressure. Release the pressure naturally over 10 minutes. Open and set the pot to Sauté mode, allow it to simmer. Enjoy!

Nutrition:

Calories: 330 kcal
Total Fat: 10 g
Saturated Fat: 1 g

Cholesterol: 0 mg
Sodium: 0 mg
Total Carbs: 3 g

Fiber: 1 g
Sugar: 1 g
Protein: 10 g

44. Shrimp With Beans

Preparation Time: 10 minutes

Cooking Time: 10 minutes

Servings: 4

Ingredients:

A pinch of Salt

2 tablespoons Olive oil
2 tablespoons Soy sauce

1 lb. Shrimp, peeled and deveined
½ lb. Green beans, washed and trimmed

Directions:

Heat oil in a pan over medium-high heat. Add beans to the pan and sauté for 5-6 minutes or until tender. Remove pan from heat and set aside. Add shrimp in the same pan and cook for 2-3 minutes each side. Return beans to the pan along with soy sauce. Stir well and cook until shrimp is done. Season with salt and serve.

Nutrition:

Calories: 217 kcal
Total Fat: 9 g
Saturated Fat: 1.6 g

Cholesterol: 0 mg
Sodium: 0 mg
Total Carbs: 6.4 g

Fiber: 2 g
Sugar: 0.9 g
Protein: 27.4 g

45. Broccoli Fritters

Preparation Time: 10 minutes

Cooking Time: 15 minutes

Servings: 4

Ingredients:

Salt and Pepper
2 tablespoon Olive oil

3 cups broccoli florets
½ cup flour, gluten-free

1 large egg, lightly beaten
1/3 cup parmesan cheese, grated

Directions:

Steam broccoli florets until tender. Let it cool completely and chop. In a bowl, add egg, cheese, flour, pepper, and salt. Mix well. Add chopped broccoli into the egg mixture and mix well. If the mixture is too dry, then add a tablespoon of water. Heat the olive oil in a pan over medium heat. Make patties from the mixture and cook on the hot pan for 3 minutes each side. Serve and enjoy.

Nutrition:

Calories: 208 kcal
Total Fat: 11.6 g
Saturated Fat: 3.4 g

Cholesterol: 0 mg
Sodium: 0 mg
Total Carbs: 16.6 g

Fiber: 2.2 g
Sugar: 1.3 g
Protein: 9.1 g

46. Roasted Broccoli

Preparation Time: 10 minutes

Cooking Time: 15 minutes

Servings: 8

Ingredients:

¼ cup olive oil
8 cups broccoli florets
2 tablespoon Soy sauce
½ teaspoon red chili flakes

Directions:

Preheat the oven to 425°F. Spray a baking tray with cooking spray and set aside. Add all ingredients to the large mixing bowl and toss well. Transfer broccoli mixture on a prepared baking tray. Roast in preheated oven for 15 minutes. Serve and enjoy.

Nutrition:

Calories: 87 kcal
Total Fat: 6.6 g
Saturated Fat: 0.9 g

Cholesterol: 0 mg
Sodium: 0 mg
Total Carbs: 6.3 g

Fiber: 2.4 g
Sugar: 1.6 g
Protein: 2.8 g

47. Roasted Maple Carrots

Preparation Time: 10 minutes

Cooking Time: 25 minutes

Servings: 3

Ingredients:

Salt and Pepper
1 lb. Baby carrots

3 tablespoons Maple syrup
1 tablespoon Dijon mustard

2 tablespoons Butter, melted
2 teaspoon fresh parsley, chopped

Directions:

Preheat the oven to 400 °F. In a large bowl, toss carrots with dijon mustard, maple syrup, butter, pepper, and salt. Transfer carrots to baking tray and spread evenly. Roast carrots in preheated oven for 25-30 minutes. Serve and enjoy.

Nutrition:

Calories: 177 kcal
Total Fat: 8.1 g
Saturated Fat: 4.9 g

Cholesterol: 0 mg
Sodium: 0 mg
Total Carbs: 26.2 g

Fiber: 4.6 g
Sugar: 19.2 g
Protein: 1.3 g

48. Sweet & Tangy Green Beans

Preparation Time: 10 minutes

Cooking Time: 15 minutes

Servings: 5

Ingredients:

¼ cup olive oil
Salt and Pepper

½ cup pecans, chopped
1 tablespoon Maple syrup

2 tablespoons Dijon mustard
1 ½ lbs. Green beans, trimmed
2 tablespoons Rice wine vinegar

Directions:

Preheat the oven to 400°F. Place pecans on baking tray and toast in preheated oven for 5-8 minutes. Remove from oven and let it cool. Boil water in a large pot over high heat. Add green beans in boiling water and cook for 4-5 minutes or until tender. Drain beans well and place in a large bowl. In a small bowl, whisk together oil, maple syrup, mustard, and vinegar. Season beans with pepper and salt. Pour oil mixture over green beans. Add pecans and toss well. Serve and enjoy.

Nutrition:

Calories: 139 kcal
Total Fat: 10.4 g
Saturated Fat: 1.4 g

Cholesterol: 0 mg
Sodium: 0 mg
Total Carbs: 10.9 g

Fiber: 4.3 g
Sugar: 3.7 g
Protein: 2.5 g

49. Easy Lemon Chicken

 Preparation Time: 5 minutes   **Cooking Time:** 15 minutes   **Servings:** 1

Ingredients:

Salt and Pepper

1 fresh lemon juice
1 fresh lemon, sliced

1/2 tablespoon Italian seasoning
1 chicken breast, boneless and skinless

Directions:

Preheat the oven to 350°F. Season chicken with Italian season, pepper and salt. Place chicken breast onto the foil piece. Pour lemon juice over chicken and arrange lemon slices on top of chicken. Tightly fold foil around the chicken breast and place in air fryer basket and cook for 15 minutes. Serve and enjoy.

Nutrition:

Calories: 179
Total Fat: 5.5g
Sugar: 3.1g

Saturated Fat: 0.7g
Protein: 25.1g

Carbs: 7.2g
Fiber: 1.8g

50. Flavorful Greek Chicken

Preparation Time: 10 minutes

Cooking Time: 10 minutes

Servings: 6

Ingredients:

1/2 cup olives
Salt and Pepper
1/2 teaspoon paprika
900 grams chicken thighs, skinless and boneless

2 tablespoons olive oil
28 oz can tomato, diced
2 teaspoons dried parsley

3/4 teaspoon chili pepper
2 teaspoons dried oregano
1/2 teaspoon ground coriander

Directions:

Add oil in the instant pot and set the pot on sauté mode. Add chicken to the pot and sauté until brown. Transfer chicken on a plate. Add tomatoes, spices, pepper, and salt and cook for 2-3 minutes. Return chicken to the pot and stir well to combine. Seal pot with lid and cook on manual mode for 8 minutes. Once done then release pressure using quick-release method than open the lid. Add olives and stir well. Serve and enjoy.

Nutrition:

Calories: 275
Total Fat: 12.9g
Sugar: 2.2g

Saturated Fat: 2.9g
Protein: 33.7g

Carbs: 4.5g
Fiber: 1.2g

Chapter 7:
Low-FODMAP Pasta

51. Roasted Pepper Pasta

Preparation Time: 10 minutes

Cooking Time: 10 minutes

Servings: 4

Ingredients:

A pinch of salt

¼ cup pumpkin puree

2 tablespoons olive oil

1 tablespoon tapioca starch

2 cups red bell peppers, roasted

1 cup unsweetened almond milk

4 cups gluten-free pasta, cooked

3 tablespoons parmesan cheese, grated

3 tablespoons. fresh basil leaves, chopped

Directions:

Add roasted bell peppers, parmesan cheese, basil leaves, tapioca starch, almond milk, olive oil, and pumpkin puree into a blender and blend until smooth. Pour blended sauce into a large pan and heat over medium-high heat. Stir well and cook the sauce until slightly thickens. Add cooked pasta to the sauce and toss well. Season with salt and serve.

Nutrition:

Calories: 308 kcal

Total Fat: 10 g

Saturated Fat: 2 g

Cholesterol: 0 mg

Sodium: 0 mg

Total Carbs: 47.5 g

Fiber: 8.3 g

Sugar: 3.6 g

Protein: 7 g

52. Lemon Butter Shrimp Over Vegetable Noodles

Preparation Time: 8 minutes

Cooking Time: 12 minutes

Servings: 4

Ingredients:

¼ cup butter

½ teaspoon salt

1 tablespoon capers

1 tablespoon lemon juice

½ teaspoon black pepper

1 lb. shrimp, cleaned and deveined

4 cups zucchini, spiral sliced into noodles

Directions:

Bring a lightly salted pot of water to a boil. Add the zucchini spirals to the water and cook for 2-3 minutes. Carefully remove the zucchini from the cooking water and transfer it to a bowl of ice water to stop the cooking. Let sit for 1-2 minutes before draining. Heat the butter in a skillet over medium heat. Sprinkle the shrimp with lemon juice and season it with the salt and black pepper. Place the shrimp in the skillet with the butter, along with the capers. Cook for 2-3 minutes per side, or until cooked thoroughly. Add the zucchini noodles to the skillet and toss to coat in the warm butter. Transfer to serving plates and enjoy.

Nutrition:

Calories: 431 kcal

Total Fat: 20.4 g

Saturated Fat: 4.9 g

Cholesterol: 0 mg

Sodium: 0 mg

Total Carbs: 7.1 g

Fiber: 1.3 g

Sugar: 3.5 g

Protein: 53.4 g

53. Pasta With Salmon And Dill

Preparation Time: 10 minutes

Cooking Time: 15 minutes

Servings: 3

Ingredients:

zest of 1 lime
1 cup fat milk
1 bunch of dill

1/3 mushrooms
½ smoked salmon
3 cups baby spinach

1 tablespoon olive oil
1 tablespoon cornflour
1 packet gluten-free pasta
250 ml low fodmap chicken stock

Directions:

In a pan heat oil over medium heat, add mushrooms and sauté for 2-3 minutes. Add lime juice, lime zest, salmon, chicken stock and baby spinach leaves. In a bowl add milk, cornflour and whisk until dissolved. Pour mix into the pan, add cooked pasta and dill. Toss until pasta is coated. When ready serve with grated cheese

Nutrition:

Calories: 162 kcal
Total Fat: 3.1 g
Saturated Fat: 0 g

Cholesterol: 23 mg
Sodium: 43 mg
Total Carbs: 18 g

Fiber: 0 g
Sugar: 0 g
Protein: 9.3 g

54. Greek Pasta Salad

Preparation Time: 5 minutes

Cooking Time: 5 minutes

Servings: 4

Ingredients:

2 cups tomatoes
¼ cup feta cheese

4 oz. gluten-free pasta
2 tablespoons oregano
¼ cup Kalamata olives

1 cup canned chickpeas
1 tablespoon lemon juice
½ cup low fodmap dressing

Directions:

In a bowl add all Ingredients and mix well. Serve with dressing

Nutrition:

Calories: 132 kcal
Total Fat: 6.2 g
Saturated Fat: 2.3 g

Cholesterol: 0 mg
Sodium: 0 mg
Total Carbs: 15.7 g

Fiber: 5.4 g
Sugar: 1.1 g
Protein: 3.2 g

55. Salmon And Spinach

 Preparation Time: 10 minutes

 Cooking Time: 20 minutes

 Servings: 4

Ingredients:

Juice from 1 lemon
1 tablespoon olive oil
1 ½ cup fresh spinach
Salt and pepper to taste

1 cup smoked salmon flakes
1 can canned sliced mushrooms
2 cups lactose-free cream cheese
1 package gluten-free spaghetti noodles

Directions:

Place water in a deep pot and bring to a boil. Cook spaghetti noodles according to package instructions. Drain the noodles and set aside once cooked. Heat olive oil in a pan over medium heat and wilt the spinach and set aside. Using the same pan, stir in the mushrooms. Add in the cream cheese and pour water. Season with salt and pepper to taste. Bring to a boil and add in the salmon flakes. Stir in the spaghetti noodles. Add the wilted spinach. Drizzle with lemon juice before serving.

Nutrition:

Calories: 406 kcal
Total Fat: 5.9 g
Saturated Fat: 1.5 g

Cholesterol: 0 mg
Sodium: 125 mg
Total Carbs: 59.3 g

Fiber: 8.3 g
Sugar: 9.7 g
Protein: 32.5 g

56. Spaghetti Bolognese

Preparation Time: 10 minutes

Cooking Time: 20 minutes

Servings: 5

Ingredients:

½ lb. minced beef

1 tablespoon olive oil

2 large carrots, grated

1 cup parmesan cheese

Salt and pepper to taste

A handful of basil, torn

1 can crushed tomatoes

2 teaspoons Italian herbs

1 cup green leeks, chopped

4 cups baby spinach, chopped

1 ½ cups chopped green beans

1 package gluten-free spaghetti noodles

Directions:

Cook the spaghetti noodles according to package instructions. Once cooked, drain the noodles and set aside. Heat the olive oil over medium heat. Stir in the beef and leeks and cook for 3 minutes while stirring constantly. Add in the tomatoes, herbs, carrots, and green beans. Season with salt and pepper to taste and adjust the moisture by adding more water if needed. Allow to simmer for 10 minutes until the vegetables are soft. Stir in the spinach and cooked noodles last. Garnish with parmesan and basil leaves.

Nutrition:

Calories: 388 kcal

Total Fat: 12.2 g

Saturated Fat: 4.4 g

Cholesterol: 0 mg

Sodium: 491 mg

Total Carbs: 49.9 g

Fiber: 9.7 g

Sugar: 4.6 g

Protein: 24.9 g

57. Pad Thai With Shrimps

Preparation Time: 10 minutes

Cooking Time: 6 minutes

Servings: 4

Ingredients:

¼ cup fish sauce
¼ cup white sugar
1 package rice noodle
2 tablespoons olive oil
A pinch of Salt to taste

1 teaspoon sesame seeds
1 cup fresh bean sprouts
2 tablespoons rice vinegar
1 tablespoons ground paprika
1 red bell pepper, thinly sliced

2 teaspoons low sodium tamari
Freshly chopped cilantro leaves
1 large egg, fried and cut into strips
1 lb. large shrimps, peeled and deveined
2 green onions, green parts only chopped

Directions:

Cook the rice noodles according to package instructions. Drain and set aside. Heat the olive oil in pan over medium heat and stir in the shrimps and bell pepper. Season with salt to taste and cook for 4 minutes until the shrimps turn red. Set aside. In a mixing bowl, combine the fish sauce, white sugar, rice vinegar, and paprika. Add in the tamari. Assemble the Pad Thai. Place the noodles at the bottom of the bowl and place the shrimps and bell pepper on top. Add egg strips, green onions, and bean sprouts. Drizzle with the sauce. Garnish with sesame seeds and cilantro seeds.

Nutrition:

Calories: 429 kcal
Total Fat: 13.5 g
Saturated Fat: 2 g

Cholesterol: 0 mg
Sodium: 215 mg
Total Carbs: 52.7 g

Fiber: 4.2 g
Sugar: 4.7 g
Protein: 24.4 g

58. Coconut Chicken Rice Noodle

Preparation Time: 5 minutes

Cooking Time: 10 minutes

Servings: 4

Ingredients:

1 zucchini, sliced

1 can coconut milk

1 lb. chicken breasts

1 package rice noodle

Salt and pepper to taste

2 tablespoons coconut oil

2 carrots, peeled and sliced

1 bell pepper, seeded and sliced

Directions:

Cook the rice noodles according to package instructions. Drain and set aside. Heat coconut oil in a deep pan over medium heat and fry the chicken breasts for 3 minutes on each side or until they turn golden brown. Stir in the zucchini, bell pepper, and carrots. Season with salt and pepper to taste. Stir for 1 minute. Add in the coconut milk. Cover the pan with lid and simmer for 6 minutes. Add cooked noodles last.

Nutrition:

Calories: 514 kcal

Total Fat: 13.9 g

Saturated Fat: 7.1 g

Cholesterol: 0 mg

Sodium: 102 mg

Total Carbs: 22.5 g

Fiber: 3.4 g

Sugar: 1.2 g

Protein: 19.6 g

59. Tuna Noodle Casserole

Preparation Time: 10 minutes

Cooking Time: 20 minutes

Servings: 4

Ingredients:

¼ cup peas
¾ cup coconut milk
¼ cup tapioca starch

¼ cup unsalted butter
2 teaspoons soy sauce
Salt and pepper to taste
2 ounces mozzarella cheese

3 ½ ounces oyster mushrooms
1 package 7 ounces gluten-free pasta
½ cup green part of the leek, chopped
½ cup green scallions, green part chopped

Directions:

Preheat the oven to 350°F. Grease the casserole dish with non-stick spray. Cook the pasta in a large pot with boiling water and cook according to package instructions. Drain and set aside. Melt the butter over medium heat in a skillet and sauté the leeks and scallion for 30 seconds. Stir in the oyster mushrooms and peas and cook for 2 minutes. Stir in the tapioca starch and coconut milk. Allow to simmer and season with soy sauce, salt and pepper to taste. Place the cooked pasta in the casserole dish and pour in the sauce. Top with cheese. Bake in the oven for 15 minutes.

Nutrition:

Calories: 262 kcal
Total Fat: 19.1 g
Saturated Fat: 14.4 g

Cholesterol: 0 mg
Sodium: 205 mg
Total Carbs: 17.7 g

Fiber: 2.7 g
Sugar: 3.3 g
Protein: 7.5 g

Chapter 8:
Low-FODMAP Dinners

60. Salmon Fritters With Vermicelli Noodles

Preparation Time: 5 minutes

Cooking Time: 10 minutes

Servings: 2

Ingredients:

20 grams leek
1 teaspoon sesame oil
Salt and pepper to taste

1 large egg, beaten lightly
2 tablespoons mayonnaise
1 teaspoon ginger, crushed

170 grams bok choy, shredded
50 grams rice vermicelli noodles
210 grams canned pink salmon, drained

Directions:

Remove the white stem of the leeks and slice the green tips thinly. Place green tips in a bowl together with salmon, sesame oil, egg and ginger. Mix well. Season to taste. Scoop ¼ cup of the mixture and pour it into a frying pan with olive oil. Cook fritters over medium heat for about 4 minutes on each side. Repeat the process for the remaining amount of fritter mixture. Soak the vermicelli noodles in boiling water for 10 minutes. Heat the bok choy in a frying pan until wilted Place the fritters on top of the noodles and stir-fried bok choy. Garnish with mayonnaise.

Nutrition:

Calories: 607 kcal
Total Fat: 22.5 g
Saturated Fat: 0 g

Cholesterol: 0 mg
Sodium: 0 mg
Total Carbs: 61 g

Fiber: 10.8 g
Sugar: 73 g
Protein: 39.1 g

61. Sweet Red Pepper Soup

Preparation Time: 10 minutes

Cooking Time: 40 minutes

Servings: 4

Ingredients:

2 red bell peppers

2 teaspoons paprika

1 liter chicken stock

1 tablespoon canola oil

Salt and pepper to taste

3 tablespoons fresh parsley

8 slices wheat bread, toasted

1 tablespoon garlic-infused oil

400 grams canned tomatoes, chopped

240 grams carrots, peeled and chopped

240 grams parsnip, peeled and chopped

Directions:

Set the oven to 200 degrees Celsius. Slice the red bell pepper into strips after removing the seeds. Place bell pepper strips in a baking tray together with carrots and parsnips. Coat with canola oil and season to taste. Roast for about 25 minutes. Transfer the vegetables into a food processor. Add tomatoes and 500 milliliters of chicken stock. Blend until smooth. Pour the soup into a saucepan. Add the remaining chicken stock, paprika and garlic infused oil. Stir the soup well while heating over medium flame. Season to taste. Serve with bread and garnish with cilantro.

Nutrition:

Calories: 366 kcal

Total Fat: 10 g

Saturated Fat: 0 g

Cholesterol: 0 mg

Sodium: 0 mg

Total Carbs: 61.3 g

Fiber: 10 g

Sugar: 17.1 g

Protein: 11.1 g

62. Rustic Chicken Saagwala

Preparation Time: 10 minutes

Cooking Time: 40 minutes

Servings: 4

Ingredients:

80 grams leek
½ teaspoon white sugar
Salt and pepper to taste
¼ teaspoon cloves, ground

3 teaspoons cumin, ground
2 teaspoons ginger, crushed
120 grams spinach, chopped
½ teaspoon turmeric, ground

3 tablespoons garlic-infused oil
1 green chili, chopped and deseeded
400 grams canned tomatoes, chopped
800 grams skinless chicken thighs, deboned

Directions:

Slice chicken into chunks. Remove the white stem of the leeks and chop the green tips finely. Over medium-high heat, fry chicken using oil in a large pan. Transfer to a plate once browned and set aside. Place leek, ginger, cumin, turmeric and clover in the same frying pan. Fry the ingredients until a lumpy paste is obtained. Add spinach and cook until wilted. Put green chili and tomatoes in the pan and mix well. Add the browned chicken meat and let the mixture simmer for 25 minutes. Reduce the heat to medium heat. Season with salt, sugar and pepper.

Nutrition:

Calories: 375 kcal
Total Fat: 14.6 g
Saturated Fat: 0 g

Cholesterol: 0 mg
Sodium: 0 mg
Total Carbs: 13.6 g

Fiber: 3.3 g
Sugar: 6.1 g
Protein: 47.6 g

63. Beef Stew

Preparation Time: 25 minutes

Cooking Time: 4 Hours

Servings: 4

Ingredients:

60 grams leek
1 bay leaf, dried
1 tablespoon olive oil
1 teaspoon basil, dried

2 teaspoons corn starch
2 teaspoons lemon juice
1 teaspoon oregano, dried
3 tablespoons tomato paste
250 milliliters chicken stock

8 slices wheat bread, toasted
1 tablespoon garlic-infused oil
600 grams beef chuck steak, cubed
400 grams canned tomatoes, chopped
240 grams carrots, peeled and chopped

Directions:

Remove the white stem of the leeks and chop the green tips roughly. Coat the beef with oil. Season with salt and pepper. Over medium heat, cook beef with olive oil in a large prying fan until brown. Transfer beef to a crock pot together with tomato paste and chopped tomatoes. Pour chicken stock into the slow cooker. Add leeks, basil, carrots, bay leaf and oregano. Season to taste. Set the crock pot on high and allow the ingredients to cook for 4 hours. Dissolve corn starch in cold water. Add the corn starch mixture and lemon juice into the stew. Mix well and let it rest to thicken. Serve stew with bread.

Nutrition:

Calories: 515 kcal
Total Fat: 17.8 g
Saturated Fat: 0 g

Cholesterol: 0 mg
Sodium: 0 mg
Total Carbs: 51.7 g

Fiber: 6.2 g
Sugar: 12.7 g
Protein: 40.7 g

64. Spicy Beef Chilies

Preparation Time: 15 minutes

Cooking Time: 22 minutes

Servings: 4

Ingredients:

2 tablespoons vegetable oil, divided
1 medium jalapeno pepper, minced

29 ounces tomatoes, with chilies, diced
1 and ½ pounds beef stew meat, cut into 1-inch cubes

Directions:

A spiced-up beef dish for those who like to spice things up a notch and take things to the next level! While this dish might not be everyone, the daring ones will surely enjoy the kick. Add tomatoes and jalapeno in an inner pot after pouring in vegetable oil. Add in meat and lock Pot. Then set the steam release program to sealing position. Set manual or pressure cook setting. Cook for 22 minutes. Once cooked and release pressure. Serve with toppings and enjoy!

Nutrition:

Calories: 380 kcal
Total Fat: 10 g
Saturated Fat: 2 g

Cholesterol: 0 mg
Sodium: 0 mg
Total Carbs: 12 g

Fiber: 2 g
Sugar: 04 g
Protein: 40 g

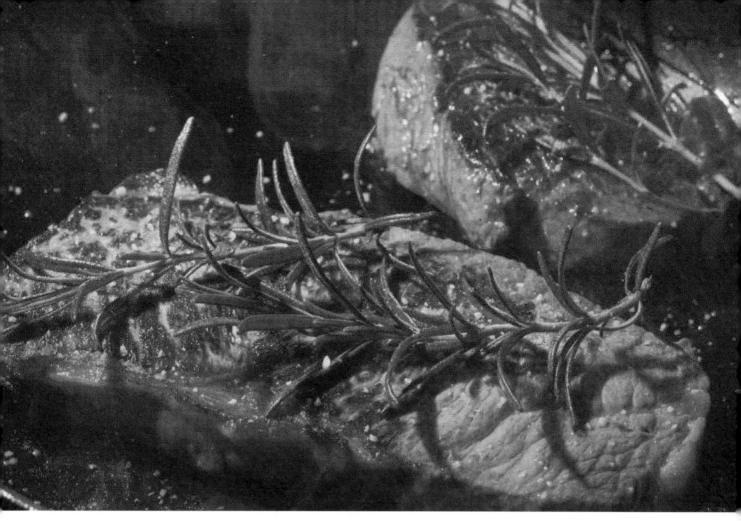

65. Almond Butter And Beef

 Preparation Time: 10 minutes

 Cooking Time: 60 minutes

 Servings: 4

Ingredients:

1 cup of water

3 pounds beef roast

1 jar of pepper rings

1 tablespoon olive oil

8 tablespoons almond butter

2 tablespoons Italian seasoning

2 tablespoons low fodmap ranch dressing

Directions:

A buttery dish that is completely LOW FODMAP friendly! The almond butter not only makes the dish creamy but delightfully delicious as well! All without breaking any rule. Set your Instant Pot to Sauté mode and add 1 tablespoon of oil. Once the oil is hot, add roast and sear both sides. Set the sauté off and add water, Italian seasoning mix, reserved juice, and pepper rings on top of your beef. Lock up the lid and cook on HIGH pressure for 60 minutes. Release the pressure naturally over 10 minutes. Cut the beef with salad sheers and serve with pureed cauliflower. Enjoy!

Nutrition:

Calories: 260 kcal

Total Fat: 18 g

Saturated Fat: 7 g

Cholesterol: 0 mg

Sodium: 0 mg

Total Carbs: 12 g

Fiber: 3 g

Sugar: 2 g

Protein: 16 g

66. Arugula Grapes Salad

Preparation Time: 5 minutes

Cooking Time: 5 minutes

Servings: 4

Ingredients:

5 oz arugula
¼ cup olive oil

1 ½ cups grapes, halved
½ cup walnuts, chopped

1 teaspoon dijon mustard
3 tablespoon chives, chopped
1 ½ teaspoon balsamic vinegar

Directions:

Add vinegar, dijon, oil, chives, pepper, and salt into a blender and blend until smooth. In a mixing bowl, mix together walnuts, grapes, and arugula. Pour dressing over salad and toss well. Serve and enjoy.

Nutrition:

Calories: 238 kcal
Total Fat: 22.2 g
Saturated Fat: 2.4 g

Cholesterol: 0 mg
Sodium: 0 mg
Total Carbs: 9 g

Fiber: 2 g
Sugar: 6.6 g
Protein: 5 g

67. Veggie Pasta Bean Soup

Preparation Time: 15 minutes

Cooking Time: 30 minutes

Servings: 8

Ingredients:

4 cups water

3 oz kale, chopped

½ cup elbow pasta

½ teaspoon paprika

½ zucchini, chopped

1 tablespoon olive oil

1 cup bok choy, sliced

½ teaspoon dried basil

½ teaspoon dried thyme

½ yellow squash, chopped

6 oz butternut squash, diced

14 oz can tomatoes, crushed

2 tablespoons leeks, chopped

1 large carrot, peeled and chopped

4 oz potatoes, peeled and chopped

2 tablespoons green onion, chopped

8 oz can chickpeas, drained and rinsed

Directions:

Heat oil in a large pot over medium heat. Add leek and green onion and sauté until softened. Add water, thyme, paprika, basil, zucchini, yellow squash, bok choy, carrots, kale, potatoes, squash, chickpeas, tomatoes, pepper, and salt. Stir well. Cover and bring to boil over medium-high heat. Turn heat to low and simmer for 30 minutes. Meanwhile, cook pasta according to packet directions. Drain pasta well and add in soup. Stir everything well. Serve and enjoy.

Nutrition:

Calories: 136 kcal

Total Fat: 2.4 g

Saturated Fat: 0.3 g

Cholesterol: 0 mg

Sodium: 0 mg

Total Carbs: 25.3 g

Fiber: 4.2 g

Sugar: 3.9 g

Protein: 4.7 g

68. Tasty Cilantro Lime Green Rice

Preparation Time: 5 minutes

Cooking Time: 5 minutes

Servings: 8

Ingredients:

1 cup cilantro
¼ cup olive oil

Salt and Pepper to taste
4 cups cooked brown rice

2 tablespoon fresh lime juice
½ cup green onion, chopped

Directions:

Add cilantro, lime juice, oil, green onion, pepper, and salt into the blender and blend until smooth. Pour cilantro mixture over cooked brown rice and mix until well combined. Serve immediately and enjoy.

Nutrition:

Calories: 157 kcal
Total Fat: 7 g
Saturated Fat: 0.9 g

Cholesterol: 0 mg
Sodium: 0 mg
Total Carbs: 21.9 g

Fiber: 0.9 g
Sugar: 0.2 g
Protein: 2.2 g

69. Apple Carrot Kale Salad

Preparation Time: 10 minutes

Cooking Time: 5 minutes

Servings: 4

Ingredients:

5 oz kale, chopped

3 carrots, peeled and shredded

1 cup apple, peeled and chopped

For dressing:

Salt and Pepper

3 tablespoon olive oil
½ tablespoon mustard

1 ½ teaspoon maple syrup
2 tablespoon red wine vinegar

Directions:

In a small bowl, mix together all dressing ingredients and set aside. Add apple, carrot, and kale in a large bowl and mix well. Pour dressing over salad and toss well. Serve and enjoy.

Nutrition:

Calories: 170 kcal
Total Fat: 11 g
Saturated Fat: 1.5 g

Cholesterol: 0 mg
Sodium: 0 mg
Total Carbs: 18.2 g

Fiber: 3.2 g
Sugar: 9.7 g
Protein: 1.9 g

70. Perfect Asian Salad

Preparation Time: 10 minutes

Cooking Time: 5 minutes

Servings: 4

Ingredients:

For salad:

1 cucumber, sliced

1 bell pepper, sliced
¾ lb red cabbage, shredded

1 tablespoon cilantro, chopped
2 medium carrots, peeled and julienned

For dressing:

2 tablespoons olive oil
Salt and Pepper to taste

½ tablespoon sesame oil
2 tablespoon rice vinegar

1 tablespoon maple syrup
¼ teaspoon ginger, chopped

Directions:

In a small bowl, whisk together all dressing ingredients. Add salad ingredients into the large bowl. Pour dressing over salad and toss well. Serve and enjoy.

Nutrition:

Calories: 148 kcal
Total Fat: 9 g
Saturated Fat: 1.3 g

Cholesterol: 0 mg
Sodium: 0 mg
Total Carbs: 16.4 g

Fiber: 3.7 g
Sugar: 0 g
Protein: 2.2 g

71. Breaded Pork Chop Sheet Pan Dinner

 Preparation Time: 10 minutes   **Cooking Time:** 25 minutes   **Servings:** 4

Ingredients:

1/4 cup milk
1 1/2 cups Panko
2 large eggs, beaten

1/4 cup vegetable oil
1 teaspoon dried parsley
1 teaspoon dried oregano
2 teaspoons onion powder

1 tablespoon garlic powder
1 teaspoon smoked paprika
Salt and freshly black pepper, to taste
4 pork chops, bone-in, 3/4-inch to 1-inch thick

For the Broccoli and Apples:

3 tablespoons olive oil
1/2 purple onion, diced

3 tablespoon brown sugar
1 teaspoon dried rosemary

1-pound broccoli, chopped
Salt and black pepper, to taste
1 green apple, cut into 1/2-inch wedges

Direction:

Preheat oven to 425 °F. Lightly oil a baking sheet or coat with nonstick spray. In a large bowl, combine broccoli, onion, apple, olive oil, brown sugar, and rosemary; season with salt and pepper, to taste; set aside. Season pork chops with salt and pepper, to taste. In a large bowl, whisk together eggs and milk. In another large bowl, combine Panko, garlic powder, onion powder, oregano, parsley, paprika and vegetable oil; season with salt and pepper, to taste. Working one at a time, dip pork chops into the egg mixture, then dredge in the Panko mixture, pressing to coat. Place pork chops onto the prepared baking sheet; place broccoli mixture around pork chops. Place into oven and bake for 10-12 minutes. Turn pork chops over, and bake for an additional 10-12 minutes, or until the pork is completely cooked through. Serve immediately.

Nutrition:

Calories 471.1
Total Fat 17.0 g
Saturated Fat 5.1 g
Polyunsaturated Fat 1.6 g

Monounsaturated Fat 7.6 g
Cholesterol 212.2 mg
Sodium 165.6 mg
Potassium 899.8 mg

Total Carbohydrate 15.7 g
Dietary Fiber 1.9 g
Sugars 0.7 g
Protein 59.3 g

72. Tasty Pork Carnitas

Preparation Time: 10 minutes

Cooking Time: 9 Hours

Servings: 6

Ingredients:

½ cup water
2 orange juices

2 teaspoons salt
3 teaspoons cumin

2 teaspoons olive oil
1.3 kilograms pork shoulder
2 teaspoons ground coriander

Directions:

Place the pork shoulder into the slow cooker. Pour remaining ingredients over the pork shoulder. Cover slow cooker with lid and cook on low for 9 hours. Remove meat from slow cooker and shred using a fork. Serve and enjoy.

Nutrition:

Calories: 693
Total Fat: 50.4g
Sugar: 2.4g

Saturated Fat: 18.1g
Protein: 53.2g

Carbs: 3.4g
Fiber: 0.2g

73. Chicken & Rice

Preparation Time: 10 minutes

Cooking Time: 35 minutes

Servings: 4

Ingredients:

2 cups water
2 cups spinach
1 tomato, chopped
1 teaspoon paprika
680 grams chicken breasts, skinless and boneless

¼ teaspoon pepper
¼ teaspoon sea salt
½ teaspoon turmeric
1 tablespoon olive oil

1 teaspoon ground cumin
1 red bell pepper, chopped
1 cup white rice, uncooked
1 tablespoon ginger, chopped

Directions:

Season chicken with paprika, cumin, pepper, and salt. Heat oil in a large pan over medium-high heat. Add chicken to the pan and cook for 5-7 minutes on each side. Transfer chicken on a plate. Add ginger, tomato, and bell pepper to the pan and sauté for until soften. Add turmeric and stir for a minute. Add rice and water to the pan and stir well. Return chicken to the pan. Cover and cook over medium-low heat for 20 minutes or until all liquid is absorbed. Stir in spinach and cook until spinach is wilted. Serve and enjoy.

Nutrition:

Calories: 547
Total Fat: 16.9g
Sugar: 2.2g

Saturated Fat: 4.1g
Protein: 53.7g

Carbs: 42.1g
Fiber: 2g

74. Perfect Baked Lemon Chicken

Preparation Time: 10 minutes

Cooking Time: 35 minutes

Servings: 4

Ingredients:

¼ cup water

1 tablespoon olive oil

Salt and Pepper to taste

3 tablespoons butter, melted

1 teaspoon Italian seasoning

2 tablespoons fresh lemon juice

1 tablespoon fresh parsley, chopped

570 grams chicken breasts, skinless and boneless

Directions:

Preheat the oven to 400°F. Season chicken with Italian seasoning, pepper, and salt. Heat oil in a large pan over medium-high heat. Add chicken to the pan and cook for 3-5 minutes on each side. Transfer chicken to a baking dish. In a small bowl, mix together butter, lemon juice, and water. Pour butter mixture over chicken and bake for 25 minutes. Garnish with parsley and serve.

Nutrition:

Calories: 382

Total Fat: 23.1g

Sugar: 0.3g

Saturated Fat: 9g

Protein: 41.2g

Carbs: 0.4g

Fiber: 0.1g

75. Simple Ranch Chicken

Preparation Time: 10 minutes

Cooking Time: 10 minutes

Servings: 8

Ingredients:

2 tablespoons olive oil

2 tablespoons ranch seasoning, homemade

900 grams chicken breast, boneless and cut into chunks

Directions:

Add chicken, ranch seasoning, and 1 tbsp oil in a bowl and toss well. Cover and place in the refrigerator for 15 minutes. Heat remaining oil in a pan over medium heat. Add chicken to the pan and cook for 4-5 minutes. Stir well and cook for 3-5 minutes more. Serve and enjoy.

Nutrition:

Calories: 167
Total Fat: 6.3g
Sugar: 0g

Saturated Fat: 0.5g
Protein: 24g

Carbs: 0g
Fiber: 0g

76. Simple Ranch Pork Chops

 Preparation Time: 10 minutes

 Cooking Time: 35 minutes

 Servings: 6

Ingredients:

Pepper

¼ cup olive oil

A pinch of Salt

6 pork chops, boneless

1 teaspoon dried parsley

2 tablespoon ranch seasoning, homemade

Directions:

Preheat the oven to 425°F. Season pork chops with pepper and salt and place on a baking tray. Mix together olive oil, parsley, and ranch seasoning. Spoon oil mixtures over pork chops and bake for 30 minutes. Broil pork chops for 5 minutes. Serve and enjoy.

Nutrition:

Calories: 334

Total Fat: 28.3g

Sugar: 0

Saturated Fat: 8.7g

Protein: 18g

Carbs: 0g

Fiber: 0g

Chapter 9: Low-FODMAP Vegetarian and Vegan

77. Ginger Carrot Soup

Preparation Time: 10 minutes

Cooking Time: 20 minutes

Servings: 4

Ingredients:

¼ teaspoon salt

¼ teaspoon pepper

½ teaspoon cinnamon

2 tablespoons olive oil

2 fresh rosemary sprigs

14 oz can coconut milk

12 carrots, peeled and diced

1 ½ teaspoon turmeric powder

1 tablespoon fresh ginger, chopped

2 cups vegetable broth, Low FODMAP

Directions:

Preheat the oven to 400°F. Place carrots on baking tray and drizzle with olive oil. Roast carrots in preheated oven for 20 minutes. Transfer roasted carrots in a food processor along with remaining ingredient and process until smooth. Serve and enjoy.

Nutrition:

Calories: 358 kcal

Total Fat: 29 g

Saturated Fat: 20 g

Cholesterol: 0 mg

Sodium: 0 mg

Total Carbs: 23.1 g

Fiber: 5 g

Sugar: 9.4 g

Protein: 6.1 g

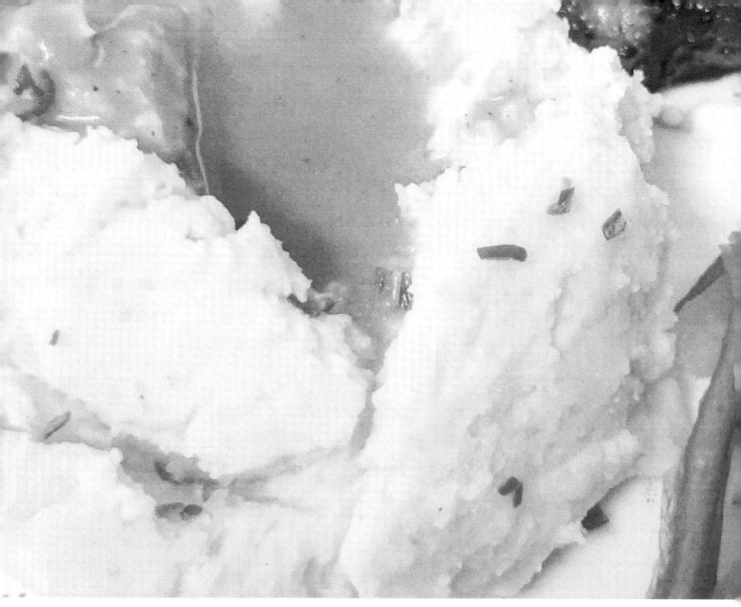

78. Tasty Ranch Potatoes

Preparation Time: 10 minutes

Cooking Time: 10 minutes

Servings: 2

Ingredients:

1/2 tablespoon olive oil

1 tablespoon ranch seasoning, homemade

230 grams potatoes, cut into 1-inch pieces

Directions:

Preheat the air fryer at 375°F. Add all ingredients into the bowl and toss well. Transfer potato into the air fryer basket and cook for 10 minutes. Shake halfway through. Serve and enjoy.

Nutrition:

Calories: 117
Total Fat: 3.6g
Sugar: 1.3g

Saturated Fat: 0.5g
Protein: 1.9g

Carbs: 17.8g
Fiber: 2.7g

79. Potato Salad

Preparation Time: 10 minutes

Cooking Time: 20 minutes

Servings: 5

Ingredients:

½ lime zest
½ lime juice
1 lb. red potatoes

½ tablespoon vinegar
2 tablespoons olive oil
Salt and Pepper to taste

1 tablespoon Dijon mustard
2 tablespoons chives, minced
2 tablespoons fresh dill, chopped

Directions:

Add water in a large pot and bring to boil. Add potatoes in boiling water and cook until tender, about 15 minutes. Drain well and set aside. In a small bowl, whisk together vinegar, mustard, lime zest, lime juice, olive oil, dill, and chives. Peel potatoes and diced. Place in mixing bowl. Pour vinegar mixture over potatoes and stir until well coated. Season with pepper and salt. Serve and enjoy.

Nutrition:

Calories: 148 kcal
Total Fat: 7.4 g
Saturated Fat: 1.1 g

Cholesterol: 0 mg
Sodium: 0 mg
Total Carbs: 19.7 g

Fiber: 2.4 g
Sugar: 1.3 g
Protein: 2.7 g

80. Fluffy Blueberry Pancakes

Preparation Time: 10 minutes

Cooking Time: 10 minutes

Servings: 3

Ingredients:

1 egg

1 cup blueberries
1 cup all-purpose flour

1 1/3 cup lactose-free milk
1 teaspoon baking powder, gluten-free

Directions:

Mix baking powder and flour in a large bowl and set aside, whisk milk and egg together in another bowl until well combined. Mix the egg mixture slowly with the flour mixture and whisk until getting a smooth consistency. Make sure batter looks like thick cream. Spray pan with cooking spray and heat over low heat. Pour a small ladle of batter on the hot pan and make a round pancake. Immediately place 3-4 blueberries into your pancake and gently press them in. Once the pancake is lightly golden brown, then turn to other side and cook for a minute. Using the same step make remaining batter pancakes. Serve and enjoy.

Nutrition:

Calories: 237 kcal
Total Fat: 2.1 g
Saturated Fat: 0.5 g

Cholesterol: 0 mg
Sodium: 0 mg
Total Carbs: 45.5 g

Fiber: 2.3 g
Sugar: 10.4 g
Protein: 10.1 g

81. Roasted Carrots

Preparation Time: 10 minutes

Cooking Time: 30 minutes

Servings: 8

Ingredients:

½ teaspoon salt
1 tablespoon olive oil

2 teaspoons dried thyme
½ teaspoon black pepper

1 tablespoon balsamic vinegar
3 lbs. carrots, peeled and cut into sticks

Directions:

Preheat the oven to 425°F. Add all Ingredients into the large bowl and toss well. Spread carrots on baking tray and roast in preheated oven for 15 minutes. Turn carrots to other side and roast for 15 minutes more. Serve and enjoy.

Nutrition:

Calories: 86 kcal
Total Fat: 1.8 g
Saturated Fat: 0.3 g

Cholesterol: 0 mg
Sodium: 0 mg
Total Carbs: 17 g

Fiber: 4.3 g
Sugar: 8.4 g
Protein: 1.4 g

82. Low Fodmap Tortillas

Preparation Time: 5 minutes

Cooking Time: 10 minutes

Servings: 5

Ingredients:

150 ml cold water
50g tapioca starch

1/2 tablespoon salt
2 tablespoon olive oil

150g brown rice flour
1 tablespoon xanthan gum
1/2 tablespoon baking powder

Directions:

In a cup, combine rice meal and tapioca starch, xanthan gum, baking powder, and salt. Cut the oil in the mix. Apply 100 ml of cold water. Mix a spoon of the flour. Gradually add the rest of the volume. The whole 50 ml, I didn't have to add. It is sticky enough if the dough is warm and sticks together. You should add a small amount of additional water if the dough is too dry. You should add extra flour if it is too wet. Working with it should be quick. Divide the pulp into 8 gluten-free dough balls. Put a slice of pastry on your table. Place a ball of dough on it. Place on top another bakery slice. Roll the dough carefully with a rolling pin into a flat tortilla. Taking the tortilla carefully out of the parchment paper, if it is not patient, it can break. For the other balls, repeat this. Heat a bath. Heat a bowl. When it is dry, put the tortilla in the cast-iron bowl. No oils need to be added; the tortilla must be baked in a dry oven. Bake on low, medium fire for 3-4 minutes, then turn over the tortilla. Fry 2-3 minutes longer. Take off the tortilla and place it on a plate. Washcloth covered with a table. For all tortillas, repeat that.

Nutrition:

Calories: 96 kcal
Total Fat: 1 g
Saturated Fat: 0 g

Cholesterol: 0 mg
Sodium: 0 mg
Total Carbs: 20 g

Fiber: 0 g
Sugar: 0 g
Protein: 3 g

83. Low Fodmap Vegetable Stock

Preparation Time: 10 minutes   **Cooking Time:** 15 minutes   **Servings:** 4

Ingredients:

Bay leafs	15 g fresh parsley	2 bushes of spring onion
2 large carrots	5 black peppercorns	2 leeks, the green part only
Half a celeriac	1/2 tablespoon of salt	Fresh herbs, like rosemary and thyme

Directions:

Cut all vegetables thin; the smaller they are, the better because they are more delicious. If you use pepper and baking leaves in a pan, put them together with the Persil, with other fresh herbs. Pour 1.5 liters (6 tablespoons) of water on top and leave the stock to cook for one hour. Save the stock and salt for seasoning. Taste again and, if necessary, add additional salt and pepper. Strain stock. The stock can be used immediately in a recipe.

STORAGE TIP: leave the stock completely refreshed. Freeze for later use in a variety of pieces. You should place your stock inside ziplock bags so that you have enough room on your freezer to freeze the bags flat on one another. And freeze it in a couple of bottles.

Nutrition:

Calories: 113 kcal	Cholesterol: 0 mg	Fiber: 2 g
Total Fat: 4 g	Sodium: 872 mg	Sugar: 3 g
Saturated Fat: 1 g	Total Carbs: 17 g	Protein: 2 g

84. Low FODMAP Granola Bars With Peanut Prune Puree

Preparation Time: 10 minutes

Cooking Time: 15 minutes

Servings: 4

Ingredients:

A pinch of salt
140 grams oatmeal
100 ml maple syrup

1 tablespoon coconut oil
50 grams chocolate chips
30 grams broken flaxseed
35 grams peanuts, chopped

35 grams almonds, chopped
1 teaspoon ground cinnamon
A rectangular baking tin or baking sheet
3 tablespoons smooth peanut prune puree

Directions:

In a saucepan, blend maple soup, peanut prune puree, and cocoa oil and melt it into a smooth mixture at low heat. Switch off the heat and leave it a few minutes to cool, so it's not too warm. Stir in a bowl, mix a cup of oats, flaxseed, alms, almonds, cannabis, and salt. Remove the mixture of the peanut prune puree and blend together. Drop the chocolate chips into the mix. In a rectangular baking tray or baking sheet, put a sheet of pastry parchment and spread the mixture out until it is about 1 cm thick with a thickness of 0.4 pounds. Place the granola bars in the refrigerator for at least four hours or overnight. Cut 14 granola bars into the plate.

Nutrition:

Calories: 217 kcal
Total Fat: 8 g
Saturated Fat: 1 g

Cholesterol: 0 mg
Sodium: 0 mg
Total Carbs: 31 g

Fiber: 4 g
Sugar: 19 g
Protein: 6 g

85. Low Fodmap Carrot Cake Energy Balls

Preparation Time: 10 minutes

Cooking Time: 15 minutes

Servings: 6

Ingredients:

45 g oats
40 g flaxseed
A pinch of salt

35 g maple syrup
50 g carrot, grated
1/2 tablespoon ginger

15 g walnuts or pecans
60 g peanut prune puree
1/2 tablespoon cinnamon
1/2 tablespoon vanilla extract

Directions:

Cut the carrot into pieces. In a food processor, add all ingredients for the bliss balls and pulse them many times to mix them together. You can also bring everything together in a bowl and use your hands to combine all together if you don't have a food processor. Take some mixture and roll it into a ball with your hands. Repeat until you've used it all. In the refrigerator, placed the balls for approximately half an hour to be set.

Nutrition:

Calories: 64 kcal
Total Fat: 3 g
Saturated Fat: 1 g

Cholesterol: 0 mg
Sodium: 2 mg
Total Carbs: 11 g

Fiber: 2 g
Sugar: 7 g
Protein: 1 g

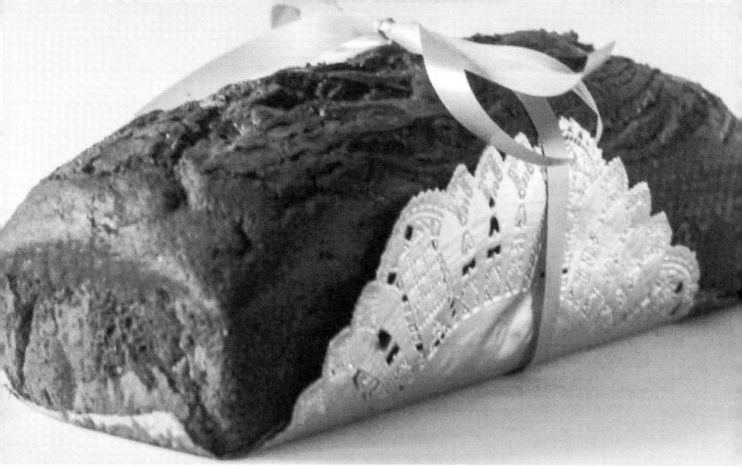

86. Chocolate Zucchini Bread

Preparation Time: 10 minutes

Cooking Time: 35 minutes

Servings: 4

Ingredients:

½ tablespoon salt
200-gram zucchini
2 bananas, mashed
150 ml maple syrup

260 grams rolled oats
80 ml lactose-free milk
1 ½ tablespoon vinegar
½ tablespoon cinnamon

80g dark chocolate chips
1 tablespoon baking soda
¾ tablespoon baking powder
1 tablespoon of vanilla extract

Directions:

Preheat the oven to 180°C. Pre-heat the oven. Grate with bread-parchment a cake or loaf tin and plate. Place all the oats in the mixer and mix until the flour is in place. Remove all other ingredients, except the chocolate chips, and blend in a smooth mix (it is all right if the mixture is made from small pieces of zucchini). Mix the chocolate chips together. Into the pot and bake 35 minutes, put the batter in it. Put your chocolate zucchini bread 10 minutes after the baking time is over in the closed oven. Switch off the oven and allow it to cool down.

Nutrition:

Calories: 356 kcal
Total Fat: 17 g
Saturated Fat: 4.1 g

Cholesterol: 37 mg
Sodium: 338 mg
Total Carbs: 49 g

Fiber: 2.5 g
Sugar: 29 g
Protein: 5.1 g

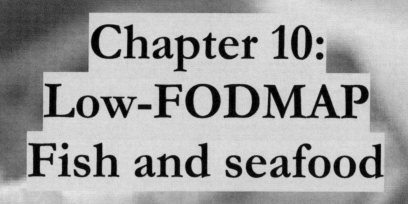

Chapter 10:
Low-FODMAP
Fish and seafood

87. Baked Salmon

Preparation Time: 10 minutes

Cooking Time: 10 minutes

Servings: 6

Ingredients:

1 lb. salmon

1 teaspoon pepper

3 tablespoons olive oil

1 teaspoon ginger, grated

3 tablespoons maple syrup

2 ½ tablespoons Dijon mustard

Directions:

In a small bowl, mix together olive oil, mustard, maple syrup, ginger, and pepper. Preheat the oven to 400 °F. Spray a baking tray with cooking spray and set aside. Place salmon on a baking tray and spread olive oil mixture over salmon evenly. Bake in preheated oven for 10 minutes. Serve and enjoy.

Nutrition:

Calories: 192 kcal

Total Fat: 12 g

Saturated Fat: 1.7 g

Cholesterol: 0 mg

Sodium: 0 mg

Total Carbs: 7.5 g

Fiber: 0.3 g

Sugar: 6 g

Protein: 15 g

88. Lemon Butter Fish Fillets

Preparation Time: 10 minutes

Cooking Time: 10 minutes

Servings: 4

Ingredients:

¼ cup butter
4 tilapia fillets

½ teaspoon salt
¼ teaspoon pepper
1 tablespoon olive oil

3 tablespoons almonds, sliced
2 tablespoons fresh lemon juice
¼ cup chicken broth, Low Fodmap

Directions:

Season fish fillets with pepper and salt. Heat oil in a pan over medium heat. Place fish fillets in a pan and cook for 2-3 minutes on each side. Remove fish from pan and place on a plate. Add lemon juice, broth, and butter in the same pan and cook until butter is melted. Sprinkle sliced almonds on fish fillets. Pour lemon juice mixture over fish fillets and serve.

Nutrition:

Calories: 255 kcal
Total Fat: 18.4 g
Saturated Fat: 8.5 g

Cholesterol: 0 mg
Sodium: 0 mg
Total Carbs: 1.3 g

Fiber: 0.6 g
Sugar: 0.4 g
Protein: 22.5 g

89. Broiled Fish Fillets

 Preparation Time: 10 minutes

 Cooking Time: 5 minutes

 Servings: 6

Ingredients:

½ teaspoon salt

½ teaspoon pepper

½ teaspoon paprika

24 oz cod fish fillets

2 fresh lemons, sliced

1 tablespoon olive oil

¼ teaspoon cinnamon

½ teaspoon dried basil

¾ teaspoon mustard powder

1/8 teaspoon cayenne pepper

Directions:

Preheat the broiler on high. Line broiler-safe tray with cooking spray. In a small bowl, mix basil, cayenne pepper, cinnamon, pepper, paprika, dry mustard powder, pepper, and salt. Place fish fillets on prepared tray and brush with oil. Sprinkle spice mixture all over fish. Place lemon slices on top of fish. Broil fish in a preheated broiler for 4-5 minutes. Serve and enjoy.

Nutrition:

Calories: 1480 kcal

Total Fat: 3.5 g

Saturated Fat: 0.5 g

Cholesterol: 0 mg

Sodium: 0 mg

Total Carbs: 2.3 g

Fiber: 0.8 g

Sugar: 0.5 g

Protein: 26.3 g

90. Salmon Patties With Caper Mayonnaise

Preparation Time: 5 minutes

Cooking Time: 10 minutes

Servings: 4

Ingredients:

1 egg, beaten
½ teaspoon salt
¼ cup mayonnaise

1 tablespoon capers
1 tablespoon olive oil
2 tablespoons fresh dill
2 teaspoons fresh chives

1 tablespoon lemon juice
½ teaspoon black pepper
2 tablespoons fresh parsley
1 lb. cooked salmon, flaked

Directions:

In a bowl, combine the salmon, egg, dill, parsley, salt and black pepper. Mix well. Brush a skillet with the olive oil and heat it over medium heat. Using your hands, form eight equally sized patties and place them in the skillet. Cook for approximately 4-5 minutes per side, or until nicely browned. While the patties are cooking, quickly whisk together the mayonnaise, lemon juice, capers and chives. Remove the salmon patties from the skillet and serve with the caper mayonnaise.

Nutrition:

Calories: 806 kcal
Total Fat: 56 g
Saturated Fat: 10 g

Cholesterol: 181 mg
Sodium: 205 mg
Total Carbs: 34 g

Fiber: 2 g
Sugar: 3 g
Protein: 40 g

91. Pineapple Shrimp Fajitas

Preparation Time: 5 minutes

Cooking Time: 10 minutes

Servings: 4

Ingredients:

8-10 corn tortillas
2 tablespoons olive oil
1 cup pineapple chunks

2 tablespoons lime juice
2 cups cooked brown rice
1 tablespoon fresh chives

Metal or bamboo skewers
2 tablespoons fresh cilantro
2 cups red bell peppers, sliced
1 lb. shrimp, cleaned and deveined

Directions:

In the bottom of a large bowl, whisk together the olive oil, lime juice, chives and cilantro. Place the shrimp in the bowl, toss to coat and let sit for 5 minutes. Preheat an indoor or outdoor grill over medium heat. Place the shrimp on the skewers, alternating with pieces of pineapple. Place the skewers on the grill and cook for 3-4 minutes per side, or until the shrimp is cooked through. Meanwhile, spray a skillet with cooking spray and sauté the peppers over medium heat for 3-4 minutes, or until firm tender. Remove the shrimp from the grill and serve with the sautéed peppers, cooked brown rice and corn tortillas.

Nutrition:

Calories: 219 kcal
Total Fat: 1.5 g
Saturated Fat: 0.5 g

Cholesterol: 0 mg
Sodium: 610 mg
Total Carbs: 28.5 g

Fiber: 3.5 g
Sugar: 18.5 g
Protein: 22 g

92. Fish Taco Bowl

Preparation Time: 10 minutes

Cooking Time: 15 minutes

Servings: 2

Ingredients:

1 avocado, mashed
Pink Himalayan salt
1 tablespoon olive oil

2 (5-ounce) tilapia fillets
Freshly ground black pepper
2 cups presliced coleslaw cabbage mix

4 teaspoons Tajín seasoning salt, divided
1 tablespoon Spicy Red Pepper Miso Mayo, plus more for serving

Directions:

This Fish Taco Bowl makes the most of just a few ingredients, with exciting punches of chile, lime, and red pepper from the Tajín seasoning salt. The coleslaw mix is a time-saver, and I absolutely love the crunch of the cabbage mixed with the smooth avocado. Preheat the oven to 425°F. Line a baking sheet with aluminum foil or a silicone baking mat. Rub the tilapia with the olive oil, and then coat it with 2 teaspoons of Tajín seasoning salt. Place the fish in the prepared pan. Bake for 15 minutes, or until the fish is opaque when you pierce it with a fork. Put the fish on a cooling rack and let it sit for 4 minutes. Meanwhile, in a medium bowl, gently mix to combine the coleslaw and the mayo sauce. You don't want the cabbage super wet, just enough to dress it. Add the mashed avocado and the remaining 2 teaspoons of Tajín seasoning salt to the coleslaw, and season with pink Himalayan salt and pepper. Divide the salad between two bowls. Use two forks to shred the fish into small pieces, and add it to the bowls. Top the fish with a drizzle of mayo sauce and serve.

INGREDIENT TIP: If you don't have Spicy Red Pepper Miso Mayo, the Avocado-Lime Crema will also work nicely.

Nutrition:

Calories: 315 kcal
Total Fat: 24 g
Saturated Fat: 0 g

Cholesterol: 0 mg
Sodium: 0 mg
Total Carbs: 12 g

Fiber: 7 g
Sugar: 0 g
Protein: 16 g

93. Scallops With Creamy Bacon Sauce

Preparation Time: 5 minutes

Cooking Time: 20 minutes

Servings: 2

Ingredients:

4 bacon slices

1 tablespoon ghee

1 tablespoon butter

Pink Himalayan salt

Freshly ground black pepper

1 cup heavy (whipping) cream

¼ cup grated Parmesan cheese

8 large sea scallops, rinsed and patted dry

Directions:

I love big, juicy scallops cooked just right and drenched in a creamy sauce. When looking for them, choose sea scallops, which are much larger than bay scallops, and avoid frozen scallops, which are harder to work with. Don't forget to remove the small side muscle from the sea scallops before rinsing. In a medium skillet over medium-high heat, cook the bacon on both sides until crispy, about 8 minutes. Transfer the bacon to a paper towel–lined plate. Lower the heat to medium. Add the cream, butter, and Parmesan cheese to the bacon grease, and season with a pinch of pink Himalayan salt and pepper. Reduce the heat to low and cook, stirring constantly, until the sauce thickens and is reduced by 50 percent, about 10 minutes. In a separate large skillet over medium-high heat, heat the ghee until sizzling. Season the scallops with pink Himalayan salt and pepper, and add them to the skillet. Cook for just 1 minute per side. Do not crowd the scallops; if your pan isn't large enough, cook them in two batches. You want the scallops golden on each side. Transfer the scallops to a paper towel–lined plate. Divide the cream sauce between two plates, crumble the bacon on top of the cream sauce, and top with 4 scallops each. Serve immediately.

VARIATIONS TIP: This recipe is very rich, so fresh flavors make perfect additions: Toss 6 ounces of fresh spinach in a small skillet with 1 tablespoon of butter over medium-high heat. Cook just until wilted, about 1 minute. Fold into the cream sauce just before serving the scallop dish. Squeeze the juice from ½ lemons, and stir it into the cream sauce before serving. Garnish the scallops with 1 tablespoon of chopped fresh Italian parsley.

Nutrition:

Calories: 782 kcal

Total Fat: 73 g

Saturated Fat: 0 g

Cholesterol: 0 mg

Sodium: 0 mg

Total Carbs: 11 g

Fiber: 0 g

Sugar: 0 g

Protein: 24 g

94. Shrimp And Avocado Lettuce Cups

Preparation Time: 10 minutes

Cooking Time: 5 minutes

Servings: 2

Ingredients:

½ pound shrimp
1 tablespoon ghee

½ avocado, sliced
Pink Himalayan salt
Freshly ground black pepper

½ cup halved grape tomatoes
1 tablespoon Spicy Red Pepper Miso Mayo
4 butter lettuce leaves, rinsed and patted dry

Directions:

Lettuce cups are such a great alternative to salad, and more fun to eat. You want to pick the largest butter lettuce leaves and fill them to the brim with yummy shrimp, creamy avocado, and juicy tomatoes. The Spicy Red Pepper Miso Mayo is a condiment I really love—a zesty vegan mayo that adds a tasty kick to every food.In a medium skillet over medium-high heat, heat the ghee. Add the shrimp and cook. (I use cooked shrimp, so they take only about 1 minute to heat through, and I flip them halfway through cooking. Uncooked shrimp take about 2 minutes to cook.) Season with pink Himalayan salt and pepper. Shrimp are cooked when they turn pink and opaque. Season the tomatoes and avocado with pink Himalayan salt and pepper. Divide the lettuce cups between two plates. Fill each cup with shrimp, tomatoes, and avocado. Drizzle the mayo sauce on top and serve.

SUBSTITUTION TIP: Spicy Red Pepper Miso Mayo is available in most supermarkets. But if you can't find it, you can make your own Sriracha Mayo.

Nutrition:

Calories: 326 kcal
Total Fat: 11 g
Saturated Fat: 0 g

Cholesterol: 0 mg
Sodium: 0 mg
Total Carbs: 7 g

Fiber: 3 g
Sugar: 0 g
Protein: 33 g

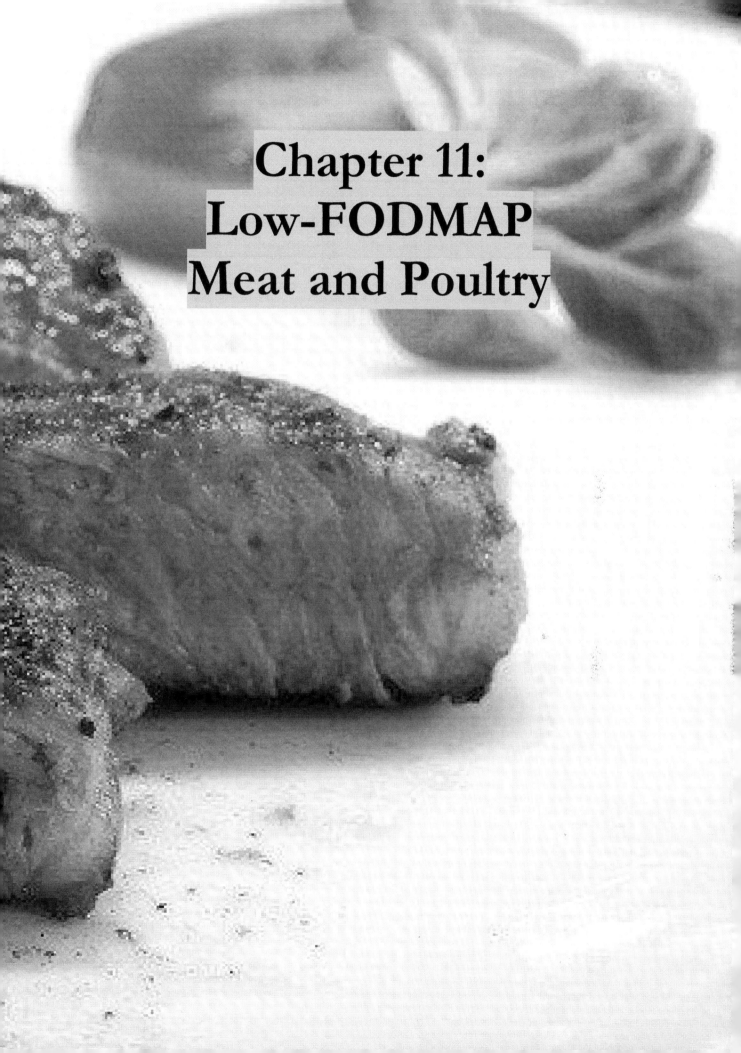

Chapter 11: Low-FODMAP Meat and Poultry

95. Beef Bourguignon

Preparation Time: 10 minutes

Cooking Time: 6 Hours

Servings: 4

Ingredients:

1 bay leaf

¼ cup tapioca flour

2 cups dry red wine

2 zucchinis, chopped

2 tablespoons olive oil

Salt and pepper to taste

1 teaspoon cumin powder

1 tablespoon tomato paste

1 teaspoon dried rosemary

2 carrots, peeled and chopped

18 oz chuck steak, sliced into strips

Directions:

In a bowl, mix together the flour, salt, pepper, and cumin powder. Toss in the beef slices into the flour mixture. Heat the olive oil in a large skillet over medium flame and sauté the beef slices until brown. Continue cooking for 6 minutes and remove the meat from the pan. Using the same pan, add wine to the pan and scrape the beef residue while heating. Place the contents in the pan on a slow cooker and add in the rest of the ingredients including the beef. Close the slow cooker and cook for 6 hours on low.

Nutrition:

Calories: 314 kcal

Total Fat: 15.2 g

Saturated Fat: 4.5 g

Cholesterol: 0 mg

Sodium: 120 mg

Total Carbs: 11.8 g

Fiber: 1.1 g

Sugar: 1.6 g

Protein: 27.8 g

96. Steak And Potatoes Sheet Pan Meal

Preparation Time: 10 minutes

Cooking Time: 30 minutes

Servings: 4

Ingredients:

Salt and pepper

1 ½ lbs. baby potatoes, quartered
1 red bell pepper, seeded and cubed

1 green bell pepper, seeded and cubed
1 ½ lb. top sirloin steak, cut into thick strips

Directions:

Preheat the oven to 400°F and line a baking sheet with aluminum foil. In a bowl, mix the potatoes, peppers, steak, and olive oil. Season with salt and pepper to taste. Bake for 30 minutes until the steaks and potatoes are done.

Nutrition:

Calories: 461 kcal
Total Fat: 19.2 g
Saturated Fat: 7.6 g

Cholesterol: 0 mg
Sodium: 102 mg
Total Carbs: 31.8 g

Fiber: 4.1 g
Sugar: 2.5 g
Protein: 39.1 g

97. French Oven Beef

Preparation Time: 5 minutes

Cooking Time: 3 Hours

Servings: 4

Ingredients:

6 medium carrots,
1 cup tomato juice
4 medium parsnips

4 medium potatoes
¼ cup tapioca starch
1 lb. beef chuck, sliced

Salt and pepper to taste
1 cup fennel bulb, diced
1 tablespoon maple syrup
1 medium celery stalk, diced

Directions:

Preheat the oven to 300°F. Place all ingredients in a heat-proof deep dish and mix until well combined. Bake the dish for 3 hours on medium heat.

Nutrition:

Calories: 548 kcal
Total Fat: 7.3 g
Saturated Fat: 2.1 g

Cholesterol: 0 mg
Sodium: 288 mg
Total Carbs: 91.2 g

Fiber: 13.8 g
Sugar: 14.4 g
Protein: 32.8 g

98. Beef Stroganoff

Preparation Time: 5 minutes

Cooking Time: 20 minutes

Servings: 4

Ingredients:

1 ¼ cups water
½ lb. beef strips
2 teaspoons olive oil
Salt and pepper to taste

1 teaspoon sweet paprika
1 tablespoon tapioca flour
2 tablespoon tomato paste
2 teaspoon Dijon mustard

2 tablespoons coconut yoghurt
1 cup white cabbage, thinly sliced
1 ½ cups green tops of spring onions, thinly sliced
1 can sliced champignon mushrooms, drained and rinsed well

Directions:

Heat oil in a large pan on medium flame. Stir in the cabbages and cook for 4 minutes or until wilted. Add the green onions and sliced mushrooms. Cook for another 2 minutes while stirring constantly. Set aside. Using the same pan, increase the heat to medium high and stir in the beef strips and cook until brown. While the beef strips are cooking, mix together the tapioca starch and paprika. Add the flour mixture into the beef and reduce the heat to medium. Stir until the beef strips are coated. Cook for another minute while stirring constantly. Add in the tomato paste, Dijon mustard, and water. Season with salt and pepper to taste. Close the lid and allow to boil. Once boiling, lower the heat and add in the cabbage and mushroom mixture. Allow to simmer for 10 minutes before adding the coconut yoghurt last.

Nutrition:

Calories: 122 kcal
Total Fat: 4.2 g
Saturated Fat: 0.8 g

Cholesterol: 0 mg
Sodium: 82 mg
Total Carbs: 8.2 g

Fiber: 1.8 g
Sugar: 3.4 g
Protein: 14.3 g

99. Lamb Casserole

 Preparation Time: 10 minutes **Cooking Time:** 2 Hours **Servings:** 4

Ingredients:

2 cups water
½ cup red wine
½ cup tomato paste

1 tablespoon coriander
Salt and pepper to taste
3 large carrots, chopped
1 tablespoon coconut oil

1 tablespoon ground cumin
1 teaspoon ground cardamom
2 lbs. lamb meat, cut into chunks
1 can of lentils, rinsed and drained thoroughly

Directions:

In a large pan, heat the oil over medium flame. Cook the lamb while stirring constantly until all sides turn brown. Add the coriander, cardamom, and cumin. Season with salt and pepper to taste. Stir in the red wine, tomato paste, lentils, and carrots. Pour in water and bring to a boil. Cook the lamb for 2 hours on medium meat or until the meat is tender.

Nutrition:

Calories: 407 kcal
Total Fat: 15.4 g
Saturated Fat: 7.4 g

Cholesterol: 0 mg
Sodium: 221 mg
Total Carbs: 16.7 g

Fiber: 3.2 g
Sugar: 6.6 g
Protein: 48.9 g

100. Maple Mustard Chicken With Rosemary

Preparation Time: 5 minutes

Cooking Time: 35 minutes

Servings: 6

Ingredients:

1 tablespoon olive oil
Salt and pepper to taste

6 bone-in chicken thighs
1 tablespoon lemon juice
3 tablespoons maple syrup

1 tablespoon fresh rosemary
2 tablespoons Dijon mustard
2 tablespoons whole grain mustard seed

Directions:

Preheat the oven to 375°F and grease a baking dish. Season the chicken thighs with salt and pepper to taste. Heat the oil in a large skillet over medium flame and put the chicken thighs skin side down and cook for 4 minutes on each side or until the skin turns golden brown. While the chicken is cooking on the stovetop, prepare the mustard glaze by mixing the rest of the ingredients in a bowl. Once the chicken has turned golden, transfer into the prepared baking dish. Brush each thigh with the prepared mustard sauce. Place inside the oven and bake for 30 minutes or until the chicken is cooked through.

Nutrition:

Calories: 487 kcal
Total Fat: 35.2 g
Saturated Fat: 9.1 g

Cholesterol: 0 mg
Sodium: 215 mg
Total Carbs: 8.3 g

Fiber: 0.5 g
Sugar: 6.3 g
Protein: 32.6 g

101.   Baked Potato And Chicken Casserole

 Preparation Time: 10 minutes   **Cooking Time:** 35 minutes   **Servings:** 4

Ingredients:

½ cup coconut cream
salt and pepper to taste
1 ½ cups cheddar cheese, grated

4 green onions, green parts chopped
4 slices of bacon, cooked crisp and crumbled
4 medium russet potatoes, scrubbed and diced
1 lb. boneless chicken breasts, skin removed and diced

Directions:

Heat the oven to 350°F and grease a casserole pan. Spread the potatoes in the bottom of the pan. Place the chicken on top and season with salt and pepper to taste. Sprinkle with bacon crumbles. Pour in the coconut cream and top with cheddar cheese, and green onions. Place inside the oven and bake for 35 minutes.

Nutrition:

Calories: 662 kcal
Total Fat: 35.4 g
Saturated Fat: 14.7 g

Cholesterol: 0 mg
Sodium: 685 mg
Total Carbs: 49.3 g

Fiber: 4.7 g
Sugar: 7.3 g
Protein: 38.9 g

102. Quick Curry Casserole

Preparation Time: 10 minutes

Cooking Time: 20 minutes

Servings: 4

Ingredients:

Oil for frying
2 chicken breasts
½ cup Mayonnaise

1 cup grated cheese
2 cups broccoli florets
1 teaspoon lemon juice

Salt and pepper to taste
2 teaspoons curry powder
1 bell pepper, seeded and chopped

Directions:

Heat the oven to 375°F and grease the casserole dish. Heat the oil in a large pan and fry the chicken breasts on each side until golden brown. Set aside. Using the same pan, cook the broccoli florets for 2 minutes. Set aside. In a bowl, combine the mayonnaise, curry powder, and lemon juice. Season with the salt and pepper to taste. Place the chicken in the casserole dish and top with broccoli. Pour over the curry sauce and top with bell pepper and cheese. Bake in the oven for 15 minutes.

Nutrition:

Calories: 482 kcal
Total Fat: 33.2 g
Saturated Fat: 11 g

Cholesterol: 0 mg
Sodium: 529 mg
Total Carbs: 3.4 g

Fiber: 1.6 g
Sugar: 1.1 g
Protein: 41.1 g

103. One Pan Chicken Cacciatore

Preparation Time: 10 minutes

Cooking Time: 25 minutes

Servings: 4

Ingredients:

½ cup dry red wine
2 tablespoons olive oil
Salt and pepper to taste

2 cups crushed tomatoes
2 small carrots, sliced thinly
¼ teaspoon red pepper flakes
4 sprigs fresh thyme, chopped

4 sprigs fresh oregano, chopped
2 pounds boneless chicken thighs
1 red bell pepper, seeded and diced
2 tablespoons pitted Kalamata olives

Directions:

In a skillet, heat the oil over medium flame. Season the chicken thighs with salt and pepper to taste and cook the chicken until golden brown. Remove from the plate and set aside. On the same skillet, sauté the vegetables and scrape the brown bits at the bottom of the pan. Continue cooking for 5 minutes and season the vegetables with salt and pepper to taste. Pour in the red wine and simmer until reduced by half. Add the olives, tomatoes, thyme, and oregano. Place the chicken on top of the vegetables. Allow to simmer for 15 minutes.

Nutrition:

Calories: 591 kcal
Total Fat: 45.1 g
Saturated Fat: 11.3 g

Cholesterol: 0 mg
Sodium: 223 mg
Total Carbs: 5.2 g

Fiber: 1.3 g
Sugar: 2.8 g
Protein: 28.5 g

104.   Moroccan Chicken

Preparation Time: 8 Hours

Cooking Time: 16 minutes

Servings: 4

Ingredients:

2 tablespoons olive oil
Salt and pepper to taste
1 teaspoon ground cumin

¼ teaspoon ground ginger
2 teaspoons ground paprika
½ teaspoon ground turmeric

1/8 teaspoon cayenne pepper
½ teaspoon ground coriander
1 package 20-oz boneless and skinless chicken breasts

Directions:

In a bowl, combine all ingredients except for the chicken. Place the chicken breasts in a Ziploc bag and pour in the sauce. Allow to marinate in the fridge for at least 8 hours. Heat the grill to medium and remove the chicken from the marinade. Grill the chicken for 8 minutes on each side until fully cooked.

Nutrition:

Calories: 237 kcal
Total Fat: 10.2 g
Saturated Fat: 1.8 g

Cholesterol: 0 mg
Sodium: 66 mg
Total Carbs: 1.2 g

Fiber: 0.2 g
Sugar: 0.1 g
Protein: 32.2 g

Chapter 12:
Low-FODMAP
Soups and Salads

105.   Deviled Egg Salad

Preparation Time: 15 minutes

Cooking Time: 0 minutes

Servings: 4

Ingredients:

½ cup minced celery
A pinch of Sea salt
1 red bell pepper, minced
1 tablespoon Dijon mustard

Freshly ground black pepper
¼ cup Homemade Almond Mayo
½ teaspoon paprika, plus more for garnish
¼ cup thinly sliced scallions, white and green parts
6 large hard-boiled eggs, peeled, cooled, and roughly chopped

Directions:

In a large bowl, combine the chopped eggs, scallions, celery, bell pepper, mustard, Homemade Almond Mayo, and paprika. Season with salt and pepper. Mix well, adding more mayo if needed. Sprinkle with a little extra paprika on top and serve.

STORAGE NOTE: You can make this ahead and store in the fridge in an airtight container for 1 week.

RECIPE TIP: When hard-boiling eggs, I add a teaspoon of baking soda to the water before it boils, then let the eggs sit in cold water while I prep my vegetables to make them easy to peel.

Nutrition:

Calories: 225 kcal
Total Fat: 16 g
Saturated Fat: 4 g

Cholesterol: 0 mg
Sodium: 237 mg
Total Carbs: 10 g

Fiber: 1 g
Sugar: 0 g
Protein: 12 g

106. Carrot And Beet Coleslaw

Preparation Time: 10 minutes

Cooking Time: 0 minutes

Servings: 2

Ingredients:

¼ cup plain Greek yogurt

¼ cup toasted pumpkin seeds

1 tablespoon fresh dill, minced

2 large beets, peeled and shredded

3 large carrots, peeled and shredded

1 large green apple, cored and shredded

1 tablespoon freshly squeezed lemon juice

Directions:

In a large salad bowl, combine the carrots, beets, apple, dill, lemon juice, yogurt, and pumpkin seeds. Mix well and serve.

STORAGE NOTE: This salad keeps well in the fridge for a whole week in an airtight container.

RECIPE TIP: You can use Homemade Almond Mayo in place of the Greek yogurt to make this recipe vegan.

Nutrition:

Calories: 265 kcal

Total Fat: 9 g

Saturated Fat: 2 g

Cholesterol: 0 mg

Sodium: 173 mg

Total Carbs: 41 g

Fiber: 8 g

Sugar: 0 g

Protein: 10 g

107. Creamy Tomato-Basil Soup

Preparation Time: 5 minutes

Cooking Time: 15 minutes

Servings: 4

Ingredients:

Pink Himalayan salt
4 tablespoons butter

2 ounces cream cheese
Freshly ground black pepper

¼ cup heavy (whipping) cream
¼ cup chopped fresh basil leaves
1 (14.5-ounce) can diced tomatoes

Directions:

My parents always request that I make this soup whenever I go to visit them. The soup is so fresh and creamy, you will never want to eat canned soup again. Pour the tomatoes with their juices into a food processor (or blender) and purée until smooth. In a medium saucepan over medium heat, cook the tomatoes, cream cheese, heavy cream, and butter for 10 minutes, stirring occasionally, until all is melted and thoroughly combined. Add the basil, and season with pink Himalayan salt and pepper. Continue stirring for 5 minutes more, until completely smooth. If you wish, you could also use an immersion blender to make short work of smoothing the soup. Pour the soup into four bowls and serve.

INGREDIENT TIP: You could also use plain, unseasoned diced tomatoes, but I prefer packing in more flavor by using the Italian-seasoned tomatoes.

Nutrition:

Calories: 239 kcal
Total Fat: 22 g
Saturated Fat: 0 g

Cholesterol: 0 mg
Sodium: 0 mg
Total Carbs: 9 g

Fiber: 2 g
Sugar: 0 g
Protein: 3 g

108. Broccoli-Cheese Soup

Preparation Time: 4 minutes

Cooking Time: 20 minutes

Servings: 4

Ingredients:

Pink Himalayan salt

2 tablespoons butter

Freshly ground black pepper

1 cup heavy (whipping) cream

1 cup chicken or vegetable broth

1 cup broccoli florets, finely chopped

1 cup shredded cheese, some reserved for topping

Directions:

When the temperature falls below 60°F in Los Angeles, I always crave a hearty soup. Broccoli-Cheese Soup is one of those keto-perfect soups that make a complete entrée. Tasty and very filling. In a medium saucepan over medium heat, melt the butter. Add the broccoli and sauté in the butter for about 5 minutes, until tender. Add the cream and the chicken broth, stirring constantly. Season with pink Himalayan salt and pepper. Cook, stirring occasionally, for 10 to 15 minutes, until the soup has thickened. Turn down the heat to low, and begin adding the shredded cheese. Reserve a small handful of cheese for topping the bowls of soup. (Do not add all the cheese at once, or it may clump up.) Add small amounts, slowly, while stirring constantly. Pour the soup into four bowls, top each with half of the reserved cheese, and serve.

VARIATIONS: This soup is a creamy, delicious canvas for additional flavors and textures: If you like your soup with a spicy kick, you can add ¼ teaspoon of red pepper flakes. For additional flavor, add 1 garlic clove, minced, and ¼ onion, diced, when you add the broccoli. Crumbled bacon (2 cooked slices) provides a tasty topping for the soup. Sprinkle it over the top.

INGREDIENT TIP: If you prefer a smoother texture, you can use an immersion blender for the soup mixture before you add the cheese.

Nutrition:

Calories: 383 kcal

Total Fat: 37 g

Saturated Fat: 0 g

Cholesterol: 0 mg

Sodium: 0 mg

Total Carbs: 4 g

Fiber: 1 g

Sugar: 0 g

Protein: 10 g

109. Taco Soup

Preparation Time: 5 minutes

Cooking Time: 4 Hours

Servings: 4

Ingredients:

2 cups beef broth
Pink Himalayan salt

1 pound ground beef
8 ounces cream cheese

1 tablespoon taco seasoning
Freshly ground black pepper
1 (10-ounce) can diced tomatoes

Directions:

This soup has a nice kick of flavor from the taco seasoning mixed with the seasoned tomatoes. The base is creamy and rich. It's so rich, you could even make some low-carb tortilla chips and dip them into this delicious mixture. Browning the ground beef on the stove top contributes extra flavor to the soup. With the crock insert in place, preheat the slow cooker to low. On the stove top, in a medium skillet over medium-high heat, sauté the ground beef until browned, about 8 minutes, and season with pink Himalayan salt and pepper. Add the ground beef, beef broth, tomatoes, taco seasoning, and cream cheese to the slow cooker. Cover and cook on low for 4 hours, stirring occasionally. Ladle into four bowls and serve.

INGREDIENT TIP: Instead of ground beef, you can use spicy sausage.

Nutrition:

Calories: 422 kcal
Total Fat: 33 g
Saturated Fat: 0 g

Cholesterol: 0 mg
Sodium: 0 mg
Total Carbs: 6 g

Fiber: 1 g
Sugar: 0 g
Protein: 25 g

110.   Ratatouille

Preparation Time: 10 minutes

Cooking Time: 30 minutes

Servings: 4

Ingredients:

½ teaspoon sea salt
1 zucchini, thinly sliced
1 teaspoon dried thyme

1 teaspoon dried oregano
1 large eggplant, thinly sliced
1 yellow squash, thinly sliced

1 (14.5-ounce) can diced tomatoes
Extra-virgin olive oil or garlic-infused olive oil

Directions:

Preheat the oven to 350°F. In a small baking dish or cast-iron skillet, spread the tomatoes and their juices across the bottom. Layer the eggplant, squash, and zucchini slices, alternating overlapping slices, on top of the tomatoes, working from the outer edge of the pan to the center in a spiral pattern. Sprinkle the vegetables with the salt, oregano, and thyme, and drizzle with olive oil. Bake for 30 minutes, or until the tomatoes are bubbling and the vegetables are tender.

Nutrition:

Calories: 77
Carbohydrates: 15g

Fat: 2g;
Protein: 3g

Fiber: 7g
Sodium: 254mg

111. Basic Salad

Preparation Time: 5 minutes

Cooking Time: 2 minutes

Servings: 4

Ingredients:

1 (454 g) bag arugula

¼ cup pumpkin seeds
½ cup cherry tomatoes

½ cucumber, thinly sliced
2 tablespoons Basic Vinaigrette

Directions:

In a medium skillet over medium heat, toast the pumpkin seeds for 1 to 2 minutes, stirring frequently so they don't burn. Remove the skillet from the heat. In a serving bowl, add the arugula, pumpkin seeds, tomatoes, and cucumbers. Right before serving, drizzle with the salad dressing and toss to combine.

Nutrition:

Calories: 137
Carbohydrates: 5g

Fat: 8g
Protein: 3g

Fiber: 1g
Sodium: 18mg

112.   Traditional Greek Salad

Preparation Time: 10 minutes

Cooking Time: 0 minutes

Servings: 4

Ingredients:

Kosher salt

4 tomatoes, diced

¼ teaspoon dried oregano

¼ cup extra-virgin olive oil

1 cucumber, peeled and diced

¼ cup feta cheese or nondairy cheese

Directions:

In a large bowl, add the tomatoes, cucumber, olive oil, feta, oregano, and salt, and gently mix until well combined.

Nutrition:

Calories: 166

Carbohydrates: 8g

Fat: 15g

Protein: 3g

Fiber: 2g

Sodium: 151mg

113. Chicken Chili Soup

Preparation Time: 10 minutes

Cooking Time: 5 minutes

Servings: 6

Ingredients:

1 cup water
2 teaspoon cumin
1 tablespoon paprika

1 tablespoon oregano
2 tablespoon olive oil
24 oz can tomato, diced

4 oz can green chilies, chopped
¼ cup spring onion, chopped (green part only)
900 grams chicken breast, skinless, boneless, and cut in half

Directions:

Place chicken in the instant pot. Add tomatoes, paprika, cumin, oregano, olive oil, spring onion, green chilies, water, pepper, and salt and stir well. Seal pot with lid and cook on manual mode for 10 minutes. Once done then allow to release pressure naturally for 10 minutes then release using quick-release method. Remove chicken from pot and cut into small chunks. Return chicken to the pot and stir well. Serve and enjoy.

Nutrition:

Calories: 250
Total Fat: 8.9g
Sugar: 4.1g

Saturated Fat: 0.7g
Protein: 33.7g

Carbs: 8.4g
Fiber: 3.2g

114.   Chicken Zoodle Soup

Preparation Time: 10 minutes

Cooking Time: 15 minutes

Servings: 8

Ingredients:

2 cups water
1 teaspoon salt
½ cup paleo pesto

2 cups cherry tomatoes, halved
1 cup unsweetened coconut milk
4 zucchinis, spiralized using a slicer

¼ cup spring onion, chopped (green part only)
1 1/4 kilograms. chicken thighs, skinless and boneless

Directions:

Add chicken, water, and salt into the instant pot and stir well. Cover pot with lid and cook on manual high pressure for 8 minutes. Once done then release pressure using the quick release method then carefully open the lid. Remove chicken from pot and cut into small chunks. Add spring onion, zucchini, coconut milk, tomatoes, and pesto to the pot and stir well and cook on sauté mode for 5 minutes. Return chicken to the pot and stir well. Serve and enjoy.

Nutrition:

Calories: 484
Total Fat: 26.5g
Sugar: 5g

Saturated Fat: 11.1g
Protein: 53.1g

Carbs: 7.9g
Fiber: 2.6g

115.   Cucumber Tomato Salad

Preparation Time: 10 minutes

Cooking Time: 5 minutes

Servings: 5

Ingredients:

½ teaspoon salt

2 tablespoons olive oil

3 cups cucumbers, diced

2 teaspoon Italian seasoning

3 cups cherry tomatoes, halved

1 tablespoon apple cider vinegar

¼ cup spring onion, chopped (green part only)

Directions:

Add all ingredients into the large mixing bowl and toss well. Cover and place in the refrigerator for 1-2 hours. Serve and enjoy.

Nutrition:

Calories: 85kcal

Total Fat: 6.5g

Sugar: 4.2g

Saturated Fat: 0.9g

Protein: 1.5g

Carbs: 7.1g

Fiber: 1.7g

116.   Curried Chicken Soup

Preparation Time: 10 minutes

Cooking Time: 15 minutes

Servings: 6

Ingredients:

2 cups water
1 ½ teaspoon salt
14 oz coconut milk

2 tablespoons olive oil
900 grams chicken thighs
1 teaspoon ginger powder
3 tablespoons curry powder

340 grams carrots, chopped
600 grams. potatoes, chopped
¼ cup spring onion, chopped
14 oz can roast tomatoes, diced

Directions:

Add chicken, ginger, curry powder, oil, water, spring onion, tomatoes, potatoes, carrots, pepper, and salt into the instant pot and stir well. Seal pot with lid and cook on manual mode for 10 minutes. Once done then allow to release pressure naturally for 10 minutes then release using quick-release method than open the lid. Remove chicken from pot and cut into small chunks. Add coconut milk in soup mixture and stir well. Using an immersion blender blend the soup. Return chicken to the pot and stir well and cook soup on sauté mode for 5 minutes more. Serve and enjoy.

Nutrition:

Calories: 610
Total Fat: 32.2g

Saturated Fat: 17.8g
Protein: 48.7g

Carbs: 32.6g
Fiber: 7.9

117.   Coconut Fish Stew

Preparation Time: 10 minutes

Cooking Time: 15 minutes

Servings: 6

Ingredients:

2 cups water
1 teaspoon salt
14 oz coconut milk

2 tablespoons olive oil
900 grams white fish fillets
2 red bell peppers, chopped

¼ teaspoon red pepper flakes
14 oz can roast tomatoes, diced
¼ cup spring onion, chopped (green part only)

Directions:

Heat oil in a large pan over medium heat. Add spring onion and bell peppers and cook for 5 minutes. Add fish, water, milk, and tomatoes and cook for 10 minutes or until fish is cooked. Add red pepper flakes and serve.

Nutrition:

Calories: 483
Total Fat: 31.9g
Sugar: 5.9g

Saturated Fat: 16.4g
Protein: 39.5g

Carbs: 10.3g
Fiber: 3.2g

118. Summer Veggie Soup

Preparation Time: 10 minutes

Cooking Time: 40 minutes

Servings: 6

Ingredients:

6 cups water
1 teaspoon salt

450 grams carrots, diced
3 large zucchinis, chopped
3 large tomatoes, chopped

900 g ground Italian sausage
2 cups bell pepper, chopped
½ cup spring onion, chopped

Directions:

Add sausage in a large saucepan and cook over medium heat until browned. Add tomatoes, water, spring onion, bell peppers, carrots, and salt and bring to boil over medium-high heat. Turn heat to medium-low. Cover and cook for 20 minutes. Add zucchini and cook for 10 minutes more. Serve and enjoy.

Nutrition:

Calories: 542
Total Fat: 35.3g
Sugar: 13.8g

Saturated Fat: 12.1g
Protein: 30.6g

Carbs: 22.7g
Fiber: 5.5g

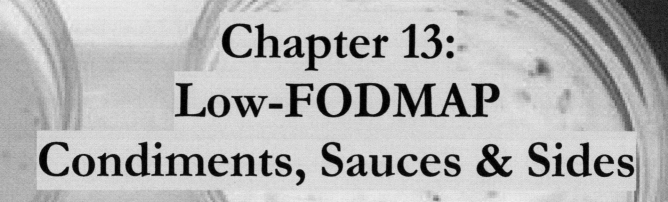

Chapter 13:
Low-FODMAP
Condiments, Sauces & Sides

119.   Dill And Caraway Sauerkraut

Preparation Time: 30 minutes   **Cooking Time:** 0 minutes   **Servings:** 2

Ingredients:

3½ cups water   1 tablespoon sea salt
1 bunch fresh dill   1 teaspoon caraway seeds
2 green cabbages, cored and shredded with a food processor or using a knife
1 culture starter (I use Body Ecology) (optional, see tip; omit for DF/Vegan or use a vegan starter)

Directions:

In a blender, combine the dill, water, salt, and starter (if using). Blend until liquefied. In a large mixing bowl, combine the shredded cabbage, caraway seeds, and dill mixture. Squeeze and massage the cabbage thoroughly until additional liquid collects in the bowl and the cabbage is not as firm. Pack tightly into 1-quart mason jars. Cap each loosely with a lid don't fully tighten. Store in a large plastic container to catch any leaks from the jars, which are not uncommon. Store at 72°F for 3 to 7 days (see recipe tip). The longer you leave the sauerkraut, the more potent in probiotic content it will become. Taste at intervals during the last few days, and when you like the flavor, screw the caps down tightly and refrigerate before enjoying.

STORAGE NOTE: This will keep, refrigerated and unopened, for a few months. Once opened, the sauerkraut can stay refrigerated for up to 1 month.

RECIPE TIP: I use a heating pad under the jars to maintain 72°F or warmer; otherwise, the bacteria may go dormant and stop fermenting the vegetables. Expect some leaking, but do NOT tighten the jar lids too tightly or they may crack. If you have a gut-related disorder, it is best to start with 1 tablespoon of fermented vegetables and work your way up each week. You can expect some tolerable bloating that should subside the more you consume them. Vegetables will ferment with sea salt only; the culture starter is optional. However, when healing the gut, it is wise to add as many as possible of the specific strains of bacteria needed to help the healing process. Using a starter like Body Ecology Culture is a great idea.

Nutrition:

Calories: 7 kcal   Cholesterol: 0 mg   Fiber: 1 g
Total Fat: 0 g   Sodium: 707 mg   Sugar: 0 g
Saturated Fat: 0 g   Total Carbs: 1 g   Protein: 0 g

120.   Tomato Purée

Preparation Time: 20 minutes

Cooking Time: 0 minutes

Servings: 10

Ingredients:

1 teaspoon sea salt
1 tablespoon Garlic-Infused Oil

1/4 teaspoon freshly ground black pepper
5 medium ripe tomatoes, cored, seeded, and diced

Directions:

Heat oil over medium-low heat in a large saucepan. Add tomatoes to oil and stir. Season with salt and pepper. Sauté, stirring occasionally, for 15–20 minutes, until tomatoes are soft and broken down. Remove from heat to cool. Transfer cooled tomatoes to a food processor and blend completely. Set a large strainer over a large bowl. Transfer purée to strainer. Press down with a large spoon to completely separate solids in strainer from purée in bowl. Transfer to an airtight container and store in the refrigerator.

Nutrition:

Calories: 77 kcal
Total Fat: 5 g
Saturated Fat: 0 g

Cholesterol: 0 mg
Sodium: 795 mg
Total Carbs: 8 g

Fiber: 3 g
Sugar: 5 g
Protein: 2 g

121.   Tomato Paste

 Preparation Time: 20 minutes

 Cooking Time: 2 Hours

 Servings: 2 cups

Ingredients:

1 1/2 cups Tomato Purée

Directions:

Preheat oven to 300°F. Pour purée into an ovenproof skillet. Cook, uncovered, for about 2 hours, stirring every 20 minutes, until a paste consistency is formed. Cool completely.

Nutrition:

Calories: 22 kcal
Total Fat: 0 g
Saturated Fat: 0 g

Cholesterol: 0 mg
Sodium: 475 mg
Total Carbs: 5 g

Fiber: 1 g
Sugar: 3 g
Protein: 1 g

122.   Roasted Tomato Sauce

Preparation Time: 10 minutes

Cooking Time: 30 minutes

Servings: 2

Ingredients:

1 bay leaf

1 teaspoon salt

11/2 pounds fresh tomatoes, cored, seeded and diced

2 tablespoons Garlic-Infused Oil

1/8 teaspoon crushed red pepper

Directions:

Preheat oven to 400°F. Line a roasting pan with parchment paper. Place all ingredients in a medium bowl and toss to thoroughly combine. Transfer to roasting pan and spread tomatoes in one thin layer. Roast for 20 minutes, tossing halfway through. Remove and discard bay leaf. Transfer to a bowl and stir.

Nutrition:

Calories: 90 kcal

Total Fat: 7 g

Saturated Fat: 0 g

Cholesterol: 0 mg

Sodium: 600 mg

Total Carbs: 7 g

Fiber: 2 g

Sugar: 4 g

Protein: 1 g

123.   Sun Dried Tomatoes

Preparation Time: 5 minutes

Cooking Time: 5 Hours

Servings: 2

Ingredients:

2 cups cherry tomatoes, sliced lengthwise   Sea salt

Directions:

Preheat the oven to 200°F. Line a baking sheet with parchment paper. Place the sliced tomatoes cut-side up on the baking sheet. Lightly pat them dry with a paper towel. Sprinkle them with some salt. Bake for 5 hours, or until dried and wrinkled.

MAKE-AHEAD TIP: Store in an airtight container in the refrigerator for up to 3 weeks.

Nutrition:

Calories: 2   Fat: 0g; Protein: 0g   Sodium: 8g
Carbohydrates: 0g   Fiber: 0g

124.   Homemade Ketchup

Preparation Time: 5 minutes

Cooking Time: 20 minutes

Servings: 2

Ingredients:

1 cup water
¼ cup maple syrup

2 teaspoons sea salt
1 tablespoon raw sugar

¼ cup apple cider vinegar
2 (6-ounce) cans tomato paste

Directions:

In a medium saucepan over medium heat, whisk together the tomato paste, water, vinegar, maple syrup, sugar, and salt until the sauce begins to boil. Reduce the heat to a simmer and cook, stirring constantly, for 15 to 20 minutes.

MAKE-AHEAD TIP: This ketchup will last in an airtight container for up to 1 month. Ketch-up later!

Nutrition:

Calories: 17
Carbohydrates: 4g

Fat: 0g
Protein: 1g

Fiber: 0g
Sodium: 128mg

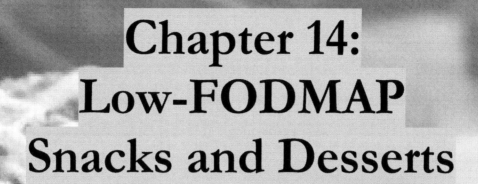

Chapter 14:
Low-FODMAP
Snacks and Desserts

125. Low-Fodmap Brownies

Preparation Time: 10 minutes

Cooking Time: 30 minutes

Servings: 12

Ingredients:

1 teaspoon of salt
1 cup of unsalted butter
1 cup of granulated sugar

Half a cup of brown sugar
3 large eggs (at room temperature)
2 teaspoons of pure vanilla extract

1 cup of gluten-free all purpose flour
1 cup of unsweetened cocoa powder
1 cup of Low-FODMAP chocolate chips
1/2 cup of dark chocolate(roughly chopped)

Directions:

Preheat your oven to 350°F. Line a baking sheet with pieces of parchment paper. Put half the amount of chopped chocolate and butter into a microwave safe bowl, put into the microwave and allow to melt, stirring at 30 seconds interval, until the mixture is completely smooth. Remove from the microwave, then whisk in eggs, sugar and vanilla. Add the flour, cocoa powder, salt, chocolate chunks and the other half of the chopped chocolates. Use a rubber spatula to carefully fold the ingredients together, then pour batter into your pre-lined baking pan. Put into the oven and bake for 30 minutes or until it passes the toothpick test, if it doesn't, bake for 5-7 minutes. Remove from the oven and set on a cooling rack. Once cool, cut into pieces and serve.

Nutrition:

Calories: 192 kcal
Total Fat: 20 g
Saturated Fat: 0 g

Cholesterol: 0 mg
Sodium: 0 mg
Total Carbs: 15 g

Fiber: 0 g
Sugar: 9 g
Protein: 10 g

126.   Low-Fodmap Lemon Bar

Preparation Time: 10 minutes

Cooking Time: 50 minutes

Servings: 16

Ingredients:

For the crust;

2 tablespoons of water

Half a cup of white sugar

1 cup of gluten free all-purpose flour
½ a cup of unsalted butter(cut into pieces)

For topping;

1 cup of white sugar

4 large eggs (lightly beaten)
Powdered sugar (for dusting)

¼ cup of gluten-free all-purpose flour
4 tablespoons of freshly squeezed lemon juice

Directions:

Preheat your oven to 350°F. Coat or grease a baking pan and set aside. Put the sugar and flour into a large mixing bowl, add the butter and mix by hand until crumbly, then pour in the water and mix until well combined. Pour batter into greased pan and use the back of a spoon or spatula to flatten and level it. Put into the oven and allow to bake for 25 minutes. Put the eggs into a medium sized bowl, add the lemon juice, flour and sugar, stirring until smooth, then pour over baked crust. Put back into the oven and bake for 25 minutes, then remove from oven and set on a cooling rack. Sprinkle a thin layer of powdered sugar over it and cut into slices. Serve.

Nutrition:

Calories: 206 kcal
Total Fat: 15 g
Saturated Fat: 0 g

Cholesterol: 0 mg
Sodium: 0 mg
Total Carbs: 10 g

Fiber: 0 g
Sugar: 5 g
Protein: 9 g

127.   Low-Fodmap Butterscotch

Preparation Time: 10 minutes

Cooking Time: 15 minutes

Servings: 12

Ingredients:

3 egg yolks

Half a teaspoon of salt

3 tablespoons of water

40 grams of unsalted butter (at room temperature)

1 cup of dark brown sugar

2 tablespoons of cornstarch

1 teaspoon of vanilla extract

1 teaspoon of rum or scotch

1 cup of lactose-free full fat milk

1 cup of lactose-free whipping cream

Directions:

Pour the milk into a medium sized bowl, add the whipping cream and whisk until foamy. Put the eggs and cornstarch into another bowl and whisk until well combined. Pour the water into a medium-sized saucepan, set over medium heat, then add the sugar and salt, then cook for 5 minutes without stirring. Slowly add the whipped cream mixture, whisking lightly until well incorporated, then bring to a boil. Once boiled, remove half a cup of the mixture and pour into a separate bowl, then slowly add the egg yolks (to the bowl), stirring continuously so they don't scramble, then slowly pour the mixture into the saucepan, whisking lightly. Set the heat on low and cook for 2 minutes or until the mixture thickens, then remove from heat. Stir in vanilla, butter and scotch. Allow to cool for a few minutes before serving into glasses. Refrigerate overnight or for a couple of hours until it thickens. Serve with any topping of your choice.

Nutrition:

Calories: 263 kcal

Total Fat: 16 g

Saturated Fat: 0 g

Cholesterol: 0 mg

Sodium: 0 mg

Total Carbs: 8.4 g

Fiber: 0 g

Sugar: 6 g

Protein: 12 g

128.   Low-Fodmap Cookies

Preparation Time: 10 minutes

Cooking Time: 10 minutes

Servings: 8

Ingredients:

1 large egg

1 cup of brown sugar

A quarter teaspoon of salt

1 cup of natural peanut butter

1 teaspoon of pure vanilla extract

Half a cup of dark chocolate chips

Directions:

Preheat your oven to 350°F. Throw all the ingredients into a large mixing bowl and stir using a wooden spoon or ladle until well combined. Line a baking sheet with pieces of parchment. Cut out a tablespoon of dough and roll it into a ball, then place it on the parchment lined baking sheet and press it flat with the broad side of the spoon. Repeat the process in 4 above with the rest of the dough, and put the baking sheet into the oven Bake for 10 minutes or until the edges have started to brown, then remove from the oven and let cool on the pan for a couple of minutes.

NOTE: The cookies will harden as they cool, so do not be bothered by how soft they are when removed from the oven.

Nutrition:

Calories: 0 kcal

Total Fat: 13 g

Saturated Fat: 0 g

Cholesterol: 0 mg

Sodium: 0 mg

Total Carbs: 28 g

Fiber: 0 g

Sugar: 10 g

Protein: 8 g

129.   Low-Fodmap Cupcake

Preparation Time: 10 minutes   **Cooking Time:** 35 minutes   **Servings:** 12

Ingredients:

1 cup of sugar

¼ teaspoon of nutmeg

½ teaspoon of cinnamon

½ cup of plant-based milk

2 tablespoons of milled linseed mixed with 6 tablespoons of water

2 teaspoons of baking powder

2 tablespoons of ground ginger

¼ cup of cold pressed rapeseed oil

1 cup of gluten-free all-purpose flour

Directions:

Preheat your oven to 350°F. Line a few cupcake tins with pieces of parchment paper. Pour all your ingredients into a blender and pulse until smooth. Then pour batter into tins and put them into the oven. Bake for 35 minutes or until it passes the toothpick test, then remove from the oven and set to cool on a cooling rack.

Nutrition:

Calories: 197 kcal

Total Fat: 6 g

Saturated Fat: 0 g

Cholesterol: 0 mg

Sodium: 0 mg

Total Carbs: 33 g

Fiber: 0 g

Sugar: 16 g

Protein: 3 g

130.   Almost Classic Hummus

Preparation Time: 10 minutes

Cooking Time: 10 minutes

Servings: 12

Ingredients:

1/2 teaspoon sea salt

1/2 teaspoon ground cumin

1 medium orange bell pepper, seeded and quartered

1/4 cup hulled pumpkin seeds

2 tablespoons Garlic-Infused Oil

1 cup canned chickpeas, rinsed well

3 tablespoons freshly squeezed lemon juice

Directions:

Preheat broiler. Line a baking sheet with foil paper. Place bell pepper pieces on baking sheet and broil for 8–10 minutes, or until tops begin to char. Cool completely, then peel off and discard skins. Add pumpkin seeds and oil to a food processor and blend to a paste consistency. Add pepper pieces, chickpeas, lemon juice, cumin, and salt and blend well. Serve immediately or transfer to an airtight container and store in the refrigerator for up to 1 week.

Pumpkin Seeds for Health: Pumpkin seeds are also known as pepitas, although sometimes the term "pepitas" is reserved to describe only hulled pumpkin seeds. Pumpkin seeds are allowed on the low-FODMAP diet and should be enjoyed regularly, as they are a good source of protein, potassium, and many minerals, including iron, magnesium, manganese, and zinc.

Nutrition:

Calories: 100 kcal

Total Fat: 5 g

Saturated Fat: 0 g

Cholesterol: 0 mg

Sodium: 103 mg

Total Carbs: 11 g

Fiber: 3 g

Sugar: 2 g

Protein: 4 g

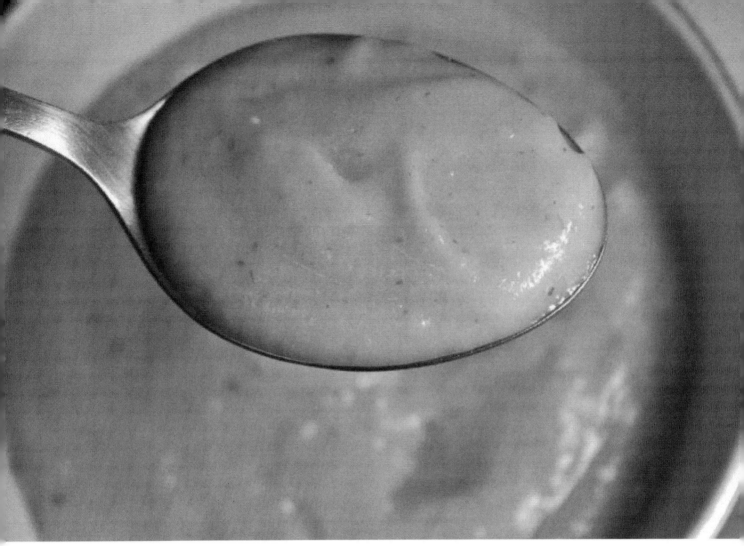

131.   Carrot Dip

Preparation Time: 10 minutes

Cooking Time: 0 minutes

Servings: 2

Ingredients:

1/8 teaspoon sea salt

1 teaspoon orange juice

1/4 teaspoon sesame oil

1 teaspoon pure maple syrup

1/4 teaspoon pure vanilla extract

1/4 teaspoon freshly grated gingerroot

1 large carrot, peeled and cut into 3 pieces

Directions:

Enjoy this dip with brown rice crackers, gluten-free pretzels, or raw low-FODMAP crudité (if tolerable) as a snack for two. Or, if it's just for you, save the leftovers and use as a soup swirl-in, salad dressing, or sandwich spread. Add all ingredients to a high-speed blender or food processor and process to a dip consistency. Add water, 1 tablespoon at a time, to achieve desired thinness.

Nutrition:

Calories: 86 kcal

Total Fat: 3.5 g

Saturated Fat: 0 g

Cholesterol: 0 mg

Sodium: 349 mg

Total Carbs: 13 g

Fiber: 2 g

Sugar: 4 g

Protein: 0.715 g

132. Citrusy Salsa

Preparation Time: 10 minutes

Cooking Time: 0 minutes

Servings: 2

Ingredients:

1 cup diced pineapple
1 kiwi, peeled and diced

1/2 teaspoon freshly grated gingerroot
1 small lime, peeled, seeded, and diced

1 small lemon, peeled, seeded, and diced
1 small orange, peeled, seeded, and diced
1 tablespoon shredded unsweetened coconut

Directions:

Getting in your "five a day" is easy when you pile them all into one delicious salsa! Serve with unsalted, gluten-free tortilla chips. For a sweeter, less tart outcome, simply omit or reduce the lemon and/or lime. Refrigerating this dish for a few hours will enhance its overall flavor. Toss all ingredients in a medium bowl and serve.

Nutrition:

Calories: 237 kcal
Total Fat: 3 g
Saturated Fat: 0 g

Cholesterol: 0 mg
Sodium: 10 mg
Total Carbs: 60 g

Fiber: 12 g
Sugar: 29 g
Protein: 4 g

133.   Chia Strawberry Popsicles

Preparation Time: 5 minutes

Cooking Time: 0 minutes

Servings: 4

Ingredients:

½ cup water

½ cup strawberries

2 teaspoons chia seeds
1 tablespoon fresh lemon juice

Directions:

Add all ingredients into the blender and blend until smooth. Pour blended mixture into the Popsicle molds and place in refrigerator until set. Serve and enjoy.

Nutrition:

Calories: 12
Total Fat: 0.5g
Sugar: 1g

Saturated Fat: 0.1g
Protein: 0.4g

Carbs: 1.7g
Fiber: 0.4g

134.   Blueberry Sorbet

Preparation Time: 5 minutes

Cooking Time: 0 minutes

Servings: 1

Ingredients:

7 oz frozen blueberries

1 teaspoon maple syrup

1 tablespoon fresh lemon juice

Directions:

Add all ingredients into the blender and blend until smooth. Pour blended mixture into the air-tight container and place in refrigerator until firm. Serve chilled and enjoy.

Nutrition:

Calories: 135

Saturated Fat: 0.1g

Carbs: 33.5g

Total Fat: 0.8g

Protein: 1.6g

Fiber: 4.9g

Sugar: 24g

135.   Strawberry Sorbet

  Preparation Time: 5 minutes   **Cooking Time:** 0 minutes   **Servings:** 4

Ingredients:

¼ cup maple syrup   16 oz frozen strawberries, halved

Directions:

Add all ingredients into the blender and blend until smooth. Pour blended mixture into the air-tight container and place in refrigerator until firm. Serve chilled and enjoy.

Nutrition:

Calories: 88   Saturated Fat: 0g   Carbs: 21.9g
Total Fat: 0.4g   Protein: 0.8g   Fiber: 2.3g
Sugar: 17.3g

136.   Strawberry Gummies

Preparation Time: 5 minutes

Cooking Time: 15 minutes

Servings: 12

Ingredients:

¼ cup water

¼ cup gelatin
3 tablespoon maple syrup

2/3 cup fresh lemon juice
1 cup strawberries, chopped

Directions:

Add strawberries, water, and lemon juice into the blender and blend until pureed. Pour blended mixture into the pan and heat over medium-low heat. Slowly add gelatin and stir until gelatin is dissolved. Once the gelatin is completely dissolved then stir in maple syrup. Remove pan from heat and let it cool for 5 minutes. Pour gelatin mixture into the candy mold and place in the refrigerator for 2 hours or until set. Serve and enjoy.

Nutrition:

Calories: 34
Total Fat: 0.2g
Sugar: 6.9g

Saturated Fat: 0.1g
Protein: 0.5g

Carbs: 7.7g
Fiber: 0.3g

Chapter 15:
Low-FODMAP Drinks

137. Low-Fodmap Green Smoothie

Preparation Time: 5 minutes

Cooking Time: 0 minutes

Servings: 2

Ingredients:

2 cups of ice cubes
2 tablespoons of water

2 cups of baby spinach
A cup of seedless green grapes

1 big cucumber (cut into chunks)
1 kiwi (peeled and cut into chunks)

Directions:

Put all the ingredients (except ice) into a blender, pulse on medium for 3-5 minutes, then increase the speed and blend until pureed and smooth. Add about half the amount of ice and pulse again until frosty. Add some more ice and pulse until the ice is broken into tiny little chunks, and then serve immediately. You could also do the recipe without ice and put in whole ice cubes when you are ready to drink. So it won't be frosty, but it will

Nutrition:

Calories: 132 kcal
Total Fat: 1 g
Saturated Fat: 0 g

Cholesterol: 0 mg
Sodium: 0 mg
Total Carbs: 33 g

Fiber: 0 g
Sugar: 25 g
Protein: 3 g

138. Low-Fodmap Turmeric, Ginger Lemon Juice

Preparation Time: 5 minutes

Cooking Time: 0 minutes

Servings: 4

Ingredients:

4 cups of water

5 lemons (peeled)
¼ cup of maple syrup

30 grams of fresh ginger (cut into pieces)
30 grams of fresh turmeric root (cut into pieces)

Directions:

Put the ingredients (except water and maple syrup) into a juicer. Preferably one at a time. Once you have gotten the juice, pour it into a blender and add the rest of the ingredients, pulse on high for 30 seconds to a minute. Serve over ice, or store in lidded jars for later.

Nutrition:

Calories: 161 kcal
Total Fat: 7 g
Saturated Fat: 0 g

Cholesterol: 0 mg
Sodium: 0 mg
Total Carbs: 2 g

Fiber: 0 g
Sugar: 7 g
Protein: 10 g

139. Low-Fodmap Carrot Juice

Preparation Time: 10 minutes

Cooking Time: 5 minutes

Servings: 2

Ingredients:

Ice cubes

4 oranges (cut and peel)
1 tablespoon of bee pollen

10 carrots (cut off the tops)
A small piece of ginger (peeled)

Directions:

Run your carrots, oranges and ginger through a juicer. Once they are all juiced, put them into a bowl and add the bee pollen, whisk until well combined. Serve over ice.

Nutrition:

Calories: 202 kcal
Total Fat: 1 g
Saturated Fat: 0 g

Cholesterol: 0 mg
Sodium: 0 mg
Total Carbs: 47 g

Fiber: 0 g
Sugar: 20 g
Protein: 5 g

140. Low-Fodmap Tomato Juice

 Preparation Time: 5 minutes

 Cooking Time: 0 minutes

 Servings: 3

Ingredients:

A dash of Tabasco
¼ cup of lemon juice
1 cup of tomato juice

2 grams of celery seed
5 grams of horseradish
Pepper and salt to taste

50ml of vodka (optional)
½ a tablespoon of dry Sherry
A dash of Worcestershire sauce

Directions:

Pour all ingredients into a blender (if it is not enough, do it in batches), set on high and pulse for 2-3 minutes. Transfer to a pitcher and serve over ice.

Nutrition:

Calories: 180 kcal
Total Fat: 0.6 g
Saturated Fat: 0 g

Cholesterol: 0 mg
Sodium: 0 mg
Total Carbs: 11 g

Fiber: 0 g
Sugar: 10 g
Protein: 2 g

141.   Low-Fodmap Lemonade

Preparation Time: 15 minutes

Cooking Time: 0 minutes

Servings: 10

Ingredients:

1 cup of sugar

8 cups of water

2 cups of freshly squeezed lemon juice

Directions:

Pour a cup of water into a sauce pan, add the sugar and set over medium heat and allow boiling. Remove from heat and allow cooling for about 30 minutes. Once cooled, pour into a pitcher; add the rest of the water, and lemon juice. Stir and serve over ice, or refrigerate until ready to consume.

Nutrition:

Calories: 76 kcal
Total Fat: 0.2 g
Saturated Fat: 0 g

Cholesterol: 0 mg
Sodium: 0 mg
Total Carbs: 2 g

Fiber: 0 g
Sugar: 4 g
Protein: 0.8 g

142.   Cranberry Festive Water

Preparation Time: 5 minutes

Cooking Time: 0 minutes

Servings: 1

Ingredients:

1 tablespoon lemon juice

3 freeze-dried cranberries

1 teaspoon lemon zest, freshly grated

Directions:

Add all ingredients to an 8-ounce glass of water and serve. Water for Optimal Digestion. Drinking plenty of water is essential for digestion. Water helps to keep stool moist and moving! If you don't drink an adequate amount of water, your body will draw water out of the stool, leaving you at risk for constipation. It is best to drink filtered tap or bottled water whenever possible to reduce your exposure to toxins.

Nutrition:

Calories: 4 kcal
Total Fat: 0.057 g
Saturated Fat: 0 g

Cholesterol: 0 mg
Sodium: 3 mg
Total Carbs: 1 g

Fiber: 0.185 g
Sugar: 0.476 g
Protein: 0.11 g

143. Orange Ginger Festive Water

Preparation Time: 5 minutes

Cooking Time: 0 minutes

Servings: 1

Ingredients:

2 orange slices

1 teaspoon freshly grated ginger

1 piece candied ginger for garnish

Directions:

Add all ingredients to an 8-ounce glass of water and serve.

Nutrition:

Calories: 45 kcal

Cholesterol: 0 mg

Fiber: 1 g

Total Fat: 0.169 g

Sodium: 5 mg

Sugar: 9 g

Saturated Fat: 0 g

Total Carbs: 11 g

Protein: 0.642 g

144. Berry Banana Green Smoothie

Preparation Time: 10 minutes

Cooking Time: 0 minutes

Servings: 2

Ingredients:

1 cup rice milk

1 medium firm banana

1/3 cup frozen blueberries

1/3 cup frozen raspberries

1/3 cup frozen strawberries

1 cup packed baby spinach leaves

Directions:

Combine all ingredients in blender and run until smooth. Frozen Bananas You no longer need to throw out bananas that get too ripe, too fast. Simply peel and freeze in an airtight freezer bag, where they will keep for 6–8 months. Frozen bananas make a great base for smoothies.

Nutrition:

Calories: 194 kcal

Total Fat: 3 g

Saturated Fat: 0 g

Cholesterol: 0 mg

Sodium: 75 mg

Total Carbs: 40 g

Fiber: 6 g

Sugar: 26 g

Protein: 6 g

145. Peanut Butter Green Smoothie

Preparation Time: 10 minutes

Cooking Time: 0 minutes

Servings: 2

Ingredients:

1 cup rice milk

2 cups kale (2 leaves)
1 firm medium banana

1 tablespoon raw cacao powder
1 tablespoon natural peanut butter

Directions:

Place kale in blender with rice milk. Blend until smooth. If necessary, pour mixture through strainer, then return to blender. Add all other ingredients to blender and blend until smooth.

Nutrition:

Calories: 205 kcal
Total Fat: 7 g
Saturated Fat: 0 g

Cholesterol: 0 mg
Sodium: 129 mg
Total Carbs: 31 g

Fiber: 5 g
Sugar: 13 g
Protein: 9 g

146. Turmeric Pineapple Smoothie

Preparation Time: 5 minutes

Cooking Time: 0 minutes

Servings: 1

Ingredients:

1/3 banana
¾ cup almond milk

¼ teaspoon turmeric
½ cup pineapple chunks

¼ teaspoon ground ginger
2 tablespoons protein powder

Directions:

Add all ingredients into the blender and blend until smooth. Serve and enjoy.

Nutrition:

Calories: 514
Total Fat: 43.2g
Sugar: 19g

Saturated Fat: 38.1g
Protein: 10.1g

Carbs: 30.5g
Fiber: 6.3g

147.   Tropical Smoothie

Preparation Time: 5 minutes

Cooking Time: 0 minutes

Servings: 1

Ingredients:

4 strawberries

2/3 unripe Banana
6 oz pineapple juice

1 teaspoon collagen
1 tablespoon coconut oil

Directions:

Add all ingredients into the blender and blend until smooth. Serve and enjoy.

Nutrition:

Calories: 319
Total Fat: 14.2g
Sugar: 29g

Saturated Fat: 11.9g
Protein: 7.8g

Carbs: 43.6g
Fiber: 3.4g

148. Blueberry Smoothie

Preparation Time: 5 minutes

Cooking Time: 0 minutes

Servings: 1

Ingredients:

1/3 banana
10 blueberries

½ cup spinach
¼ cup ice cubes

2 tablespoons chia seeds
½ cup unsweetened almond milk

Directions:

Add all ingredients into the blender and blend until smooth. Serve and enjoy.

Nutrition:

Calories: 517
Total Fat: 8.9g
Sugar: 72.4g

Saturated Fat: 0.7g
Protein: 9.6g

Carbs: 112g
Fiber: 18.3g

149. Cinnamon Carrot Milkshake

Preparation Time: 5 minutes

Cooking Time: 0 minutes

Servings: 1

Ingredients:

¼ cup collagen
¼ teaspoon turmeric

½ cup coconut cream
½ teaspoon cinnamon
1 tablespoon maple syrup

¼ teaspoon ginger powder
1 ½ cups unsweetened coconut milk
2 cups carrots, peeled, chopped, and cooked

Directions:

Add all ingredients into the blender and blend until smooth and creamy. Serve and enjoy.

Nutrition:

Calories: 249
Total Fat: 17.4g
Sugar: 13.4g

Saturated Fat: 15.7g
Protein: 3.1g

Carbs: 23.2g
Fiber: 5.2g

150.   Easy Berry Smoothie

 Preparation Time: 5 minutes   **Cooking Time:** 0 minutes   **Servings:** 1

Ingredients:

½ cup cranberry juice

2 tablespoons chia seeds
1 cup frozen strawberries

1 tablespoon fresh lime juice
1 tablespoon low-FODMAP cane sugar syrup

Directions:

Add all ingredients into the blender and blend until smooth. Serve and enjoy.

Nutrition:

Calories: 150
Total Fat: 4.6g
Sugar: 10.9g

Saturated Fat: 0.5g
Protein: 3.1g

Carbs: 21.2g
Fiber: 5g

Conclusion

It is very sure that one of the first things to do about excess pounds being dumped is a workout, accompanied by the in-depth picture of you who stand for dumbbells in the free-weights or exercise on the treadmill by the berry lookalike! Although training is undoubtedly an excellent place to begin, its usefulness will be seriously undermined without a healthy diet plan consisting of the right foods to improve your metabolism and make you feel longer.

There are many papers and journals, all preaching the same ideas about not consuming sugar, avoiding processed foods, and restricting the intake of alcohol. Most of these ideas are right and act as excellent advice, although they are much easier to say than to do! It can be not very clear—, and many seem to contradict themselves—when many people only want to be shaped and not train to become Olympic athletes.

So if you want to take shape and have any concerns about what your diet plan should be to adhere to the following guidelines, you will surely be guided on the right path.

Keep it balanced. The body uses a lot of nutrients and vitamins, so a balanced diet plan is essential to ensure it gets as much as it can. Your main meals should be an excellent blend of fruits, proteins, and carbohydrates, and some fruit between meals will improve natural vitamins and sweeteners.

Keep hydrated Most dietary newspapers, and articles emphasize the importance of water. Water helps your body flush out contaminants that accumulate as a by-product in your body; it also helps to regulate your food because your body can misinterpret being dried up as hunger, leading to more consumption. Above all, water consumption will improve metabolism by speeding digestion.

Keep the food industry as natural as possible, and it looks as if there is a new pill or a new version of an unhealthy food every week, that's now wholly fat-free and can, therefore, be eaten to your heart. The reality is that many of those foods have replaced one bad thing for the other, and the real danger is that many people are not aware of the long-term effects of the addition of preservatives and dietary pills. The best thing is to try to stick to natural foods in your diet as much as you can, so you have a better understanding of what you eat.

It's 100 percent possible to look and feel great with regular exercise and the right nutrition if you do a healthy diet plan, and the impact of any activity you do is indeed increased; more importantly, a healthy and balanced self-sufficient dietary plan will give you fat and weight loss results.

It's not a crash diet, but a system that helps you get weight loss, get fat out, and keep it away in the longer term.

If you found this guide helpful, please take the time to share your thoughts and post a review. It'd be greatly appreciated!

Thank you and good luck!

Printed in Poland
by Amazon Fulfillment
Poland Sp. z o.o., Wrocław
28 April 2022

e9bd3630-e09e-43d0-b678-3b3db37bc5faR02